Shut Up and Speak!

Essential Guidelines for Public Speaking in School, Work, and Life

Fourth Edition

John Sheirer
Asnuntuck Community College

ISBN: 978-0692689028

Published in the United States by Big Table Publishing.

Big Table Publishing
Boston, MA
www.bigtablepublishing.com

Dedication

To the thousands of students
who thought they would pass out
in the middle of their first speech ... but didn't.

Contents

Section One: An Introduction to Public Speaking

Section Two: How to Prepare for a Speech

Section Three: How to Give a Speech

Section Four: The Major Types of Speeches

Section One:
An Introduction to Public Speaking

To begin thinking about public speaking, let's explore four important questions:

- What does "shut up and speak" mean?
- Why are public speaking skills important?
- Why do people fear public speaking?
- How can you overcome public speaking anxiety?

What Does "Shut Up and Speak" Mean?

No one walks into the bookstore at the local mall and says to the sales clerk, "I'm going to the beach for vacation next week, and I'd really like to have a good book to read while I'm working on my tan. Should I buy a best-selling novel or a book about public speaking?" This book may not be one that you would want to read while slathered in sun-block with your feet buried in the sand, but it does have a purpose.

If you are reading this book on your own, or if you are taking a public speaking class, then you've either voluntarily decided to improve your public speaking skills—or you're required to do so. Perhaps you want to become a better public speaker to help improve your life, or perhaps you need to improve your public speaking for school or for your job. Either way, there's only one tried-and-true way to improve as a public speaker, and that is simply by moving to the front of the room, turning to face the audience, and *speaking*. Reading a long, dense, theoretical textbook about human communication won't make you a better public speaker—nor will a book at your local mall filled with folk wisdom about picturing your audience members in their underwear. (That technique should make you *more* nervous!) This book based on communication theory but is also purposely brief and grounded in the real world to provide you with guidance for exactly how to take on the task of public speaking.

"Shut up and speak" means that you must stop churning stomach acid when thinking about how difficult or frightening public speaking can be. No doubt, public speaking can be very hard and very anxiety producing. But dwelling on those factors won't help you as a public speaker. "Shut up and speak" means that you can't become a better public speaker simply by sitting on your rear end and studying communications theory or relying on public speaking folk wisdom. Theory and folk wisdom can be very interesting and valuable for their own sake, but they have very little positive impact when you look into the eyes of your audience members. This book gives you the guidance to "shut up" by tuning out all of the static that doesn't help you become a better public speaker and to "speak" by throwing yourself whole-heartedly into speech-making through hard work, courage, focus, organization, creativity, collaboration, and tons of practice.

Why Are Public Speaking Skills Important?

Do any of these situations sound familiar?

- Your supervisor asks you to talk about that special project you've been working on at the next department meeting.
- The first night of class, your chemistry professor mentions that every student will have to present a lab experiment to the class.
- The softball team you're coaching needs a pep talk.
- You want to make some extra money by hosting a Tupperware party.
- Your neighborhood council wants you to tell them about the idea you have for safer street lighting.

Life is full of important public speaking opportunities like these. Very few people really look forward to these opportunities, even though they can offer great chances for each of us to help make the world a better place. Isn't making the world a better place what life is all about? You have three choices when it comes to public speaking. You can run screaming into the night and avoid all public speaking and never let your ideas help to shape the world. You can stumble through your public speaking opportunities, mutter, stare at the floor, finish as quickly as possible, pray that no one asks a question, and not really communicate your ideas effectively. Or you can take control of public speaking situations and use clear strategies to grab your listeners and hold their attention—strategies outlined in this book.

Improving your public speaking skills also has some "side" benefits that make the work you invest in public speaking even more worthwhile. On the surface, improved public speaking skills can make you a better student or a better employee. When you are called on to give a speech or class presentation, you will no longer be forced to think of that aspect of the course as an anchor pulling down your grade. Instead, improved public speaking skills can make that presentation the rocket that launches your grade to the next level. And at work, strong public speaking skills can get you noticed by your supervisor—noticed in a positive way that can help you climb the "ladder of success" beyond the types of jobs where your primary public speaking duty is to ask, "Would you like fries with that?"

And when you dig deeper into public speaking, you can discover still more benefits. When you strive to improve the way you as an individual can communicate effectively with a group, you can also improve your overall communication skills. Public speaking, at its heart, is about the thinking processes involved in communication. So as you improve your thinking process related to public speaking, you can also improve the thinking processes that are so important to other forms of communication as well: conversing on-to-one, listening, writing, reading, and even understanding complicated communication processes such as those related to current events and politics.

Most important, working to improve yourself as a public speaker can also help you gain confidence in your overall abilities. The best way to improve your confidence (as a public speaker or in life in general) is to have successful experiences with the world watching.

This book should help you increase your confidence by giving you the opportunity to succeed in front of others as a public speaker. And if you can survive something as intimidating and difficult as public speaking, you can succeed at just about anything!

Why do People Fear Public Speaking?

What is so frightening about public speaking? Why does your mouth suddenly go dry, your throat tighten, your face get hot, and your knees buckle when you have to address a group of people? Being anxious about public speaking is very natural and to be expected. If you are nervous about giving a speech, you are certainly not alone. The old story goes that more people are afraid of public speaking than they are of *death*. Think about that for a moment. That means that many people at a funeral would prefer to be the person lying in the casket than the person standing up to deliver the eulogy. That's fear!

There are four basic forms of public speaking fear. All potential public speakers experience at least one of these fears, and many people suffer from all four.

Four basic forms of public speaking fear:

- Fear of the unknown
- Fear of being the center of attention
- Fear of failure
- Fear of rejection

Fear of the unknown: If you've never been on a roller coaster, it's easy to be afraid of the extreme loops and turns. Those things look really frightening the first time you see one. Similarly, speaking in public is often an unknown experience for most people—an experience that also looks pretty scary. You might have done your best to avoid speaking in public throughout your life, hiding in the back of the classroom or studying your shoelaces when the boss asks for a volunteer, so you don't really know what it's like. Even people who have been forced by circumstances to speak in public a few times will try their best to block the experience from memory—returning it to the realm of the unknown.

Suppose you went through high school presenting only one or two unavoidable book reports, while other people participated in debates or drama club and hardly seemed nervous at all. Then in college, you consistently avoided classes that required presentations or speeches. Maybe once or twice, you had to introduce yourself to the class and tell them your major and hometown, but only when you couldn't avoid it. At work, you've been able to do your job well, sit quietly at meetings, and get by very nicely without ever having to say much to anyone except your friends and your immediate supervisor. There is nothing morally wrong with this pattern of behavior, but it makes public speaking as much an unknown as the invisible monsters under our beds when we were kids—and just as frightening.

Fear of being the center of attention: We all know some people who like being the center of attention—at a party or when playing a sport for example. But even those people often experience anxiety when they have to be the center of attention in other contexts, such as at an important meeting or in front of a class. Being the center of attention means people are focused on you—your body, face, movements, clothes, voice—all those vulnerable aspects that can make even the most secure person feel self-conscious.

You are able to walk down a crowded street in relative calm among scores of other people because you assume that no one is staring at you. You can think about your family, your job, your friends, or even what was on television last night. But the minute someone makes eye-contact with you, you tend to squirm a bit until that person looks away. Imagine if everyone on the street stared at you as you walked by. Most of us would be tempted to duck into the nearest coffee shop and hide.

Public speaking is the ultimate reason to squirm because all eyes are focused on you and only you.

Fear of failure: When someone is learning to juggle, it's very natural that he or she will drop the balls pretty often. The nice thing about learning to juggle is that you can do it in the privacy of your own home with the shades drawn. But imagine if you had to learn to juggle in our nation's capital before a joint session of Congress. Dropping balls with the eyes of 535 elected representatives glued to you would give your failure a somewhat higher stake.

That's how public speaking can be—the risk of failure with everyone watching. Public speaking failure can take many forms, from forgetting what you wanted to say, to accidentally saying something offensive, to sneezing on the audience. The list is endless. Things we barely think about in our private life (such as slobbering, forgetting to button a blouse, having a pen mark on the face, for example) take on a magnified significance when we are the object of countless staring eyes while giving a speech. These failures are actually extremely rare in public speaking, but we all feel that we are destined for such failure when it is our turn to speak, and that can cause tremendous anxiety.

Fear of rejection: Our fear of failure can often lead to the most serious of public speaking fear—fear of rejection. What we all really fear is that our messy hair or missed button or mispronounced word will lead our audience to decide that we are simply not worth their time and attention. Worse yet, public speaking can be such a complex communication task that we fear rejection because of the most common and most damaging of all failures—simply failing to get our point across to the audience. Public speaking is sort of like having a blind date with a room full of people. Who wouldn't be nervous about possible rejection?

When you propose a new marketing idea, you might fear your boss will reject your message to such a degree that you will be fired on the spot. Or you might fear that the teacher will take you aside after a presentation, hand you a drop slip, and tell you that you have no business being in the class. Just because these fears are irrational and this level of rejection is extremely unlikely, it is still common for all of us to imagine the worst possible outcome of our speech— complete rejection—and fully expect it to happen.

How can you Manage
Public Speaking Anxiety?

Any discussion of what a speaker can do about public speaking anxiety must begin with one essential premise: *No one ever completely overcomes the fear of public speaking.* People who say that they are not in some way afraid of public speaking are not being completely honest with you or with themselves. Even the most experienced and talented public speakers still feel a little flip in the stomach or a blush in the face before giving a speech. So it's no wonder average people with little public speaking experience feel as if their face is on fire and a full circus is training in their midsection.

All of us have strategies for dealing with anxiety on a *short-term* basis: breathing deeply, picturing peaceful places, meditating, exercising, even taking anti-anxiety medication. Short-term strategies are valuable, of course, but the best public speakers have learned to manage anxiety through *long-term* strategies. There are no instant cures for public speaking anxiety, but anyone who wants to become a more skilled, less fearful public speaker can use these strategies to manage the inevitable anxiety.

Five long-term strategies for dealing with public speaking anxiety:

- Expectation
- Preparation
- Practice
- Feedback
- Experience

Expectation: No one ever gives the "perfect" speech, so you should accept right from the beginning

---

that your speech will not be perfect. You won't say every word or phrase exactly right, with exactly the proper emphasis. Every hair will not be perfectly in place. The audience won't rise for a spontaneous ovation every time. Perfection should not be your goal, but you should fully expect to develop the ability to give an *effective* speech, one that doesn't need to be perfect. Removing the expectation of perfection can go a long way toward overcoming public speaking fear.

Preparation: The actual time spent in front of an audience giving a speech is just the tip of an iceberg approximately the size of New Jersey compared with the time needed to prepare a speech effectively—the old-fashioned work of thinking, researching, writing, and revising. This book presents useful strategies for building a speech so that you will be confident in knowing what you have to say. Preparing your speech content effectively can help boost your confidence and lessen your fear of failing to get your ideas across to your audience.

Practice: The first time you actually perform any particular speech should not be when you are in front of an audience making the speech "for real." "Winging it" mostly just works for birds. A very small percentage of people can actually give strong speeches of the cuff without a great deal of practice—regardless of what they might tell you. If you prepare your speech well in advance of the day you are giving it, then practice the speech as many times as you can, you will be less likely to experience fear of the unknown. You can practice your speech anywhere: in the shower, the car, the restroom, your bed—especially in the room where you will actually give the speech if you can. With enough practice, your speech will be an old friend, not the monster under the bed.

Feedback: Practicing alone can help you know your speech, but that isn't always enough. If you practice before a substitute audience, you will be more comfortable when you face the real audience for the real speech. Effective speakers often practice speeches in front of family members and friends. If you have to speak to a large group of co-workers, try the speech out on a few of your closest work friends. Or practice with a couple of classmates you trust before you give a speech to the whole class. Most important, encourage your practice audiences to give you feedback—their observations about your speech, what they liked as well as what could be improved. (You can also use the feedback form provided in Section Three to get more formal feedback from your practice audience.)

Don't settle for "that was good," a perfectly understandable comment from friends trying to be nice. Probe for a more specific and useful response by asking questions about your speech. You also might need to thicken your skin just a bit and learn to separate useless and even hurtful digs from more constructive criticism—don't lose friends over your speech. But it's always much better to get constructive criticism from a practice audience before the speech than to suffer the barbs of negative comments later from the real audience.

Experience: Most important, don't avoid public speaking situations—embrace them. The more experience you have with all sorts of public speaking, the better you will be at dealing with public speaking anxiety. Seek out opportunities at work for presenting information to clients or coworkers. Sign up for the classes that you know involve public speaking. Managing speech anxiety is a leap of faith and takes time (often longer than one semester of class or a few presentations at your job), but it's important to trust that the fear will lessen as you gain more experience.

Section Two:
How to Prepare for a Speech

You may have a few months to prepare a speech, or a few days, or even just a few minutes. Whatever the case, you should follow a plan like this one to make the most of your preparation time:

A plan for preparing a speech:

- Selecting the type of speech
- Selecting a topic
- Analyzing your audience
- Generating information
- Organizing information
- Practicing the speech
- Evaluating your developing speech
- Visualizing yourself doing the speech well

Selecting the Type of Speech

The first task you should take on is deciding what general type of speech you need to do. There are six basic types of speeches:

The six basic types of speeches:

- Introduction speech
- "Show-and-tell" speech
- Demonstration speech
- Persuasion speech

- Impromptu speech
- Manuscript speech

(Section Four of this book gives detailed guidance on and explanations of these types of speeches.)

Your type of speech may already be decided for you. For example, if your teacher wants you to demonstrate a lab experiment, then you can assume a demonstration speech is called for. But you may have more latitude in the type of speech you will be doing. In that case, select the type of speech that seems most appropriate to your circumstances. Or as you develop your range as a public speaker, select the type of speech that you have had the most success with in the past.

If you are unsure of the type of speech you should be doing, here are some test questions to help you decide:

- Are you telling your audience about someone? (introduction speech)
- Are you explaining something? ("show-and-tell" speech)
- Are you showing how to do something? (demonstration speech)
- Are you trying to influence or convince your audience? (persuasion speech)
- Are you required to speak with little or no preparation time? (impromptu speech)
- Are you reading word-for-word something that has already been written? (manuscript speech)

Not every speech will be a perfect fit with one of these six speech types. There is a great deal of interplay and overlap among the types of speeches, just as there is a great deal of interplay between what makes a basketball player a guard, forward, or center. Many players are "swing" players who slip from position to position depending on the situation. Similarly, a "show-and-tell" speech might have elements of persuasion, or an impromptu speech might involve introducing someone. But being conscious of speech types can help you keep a speech focused on a clear purpose, and learning to be comfortable with these six different types of speeches can help you adapt by "swinging" between them as the public speaking situation dictates.

The guidance on delivering different types of speeches in Section Four can be especially beneficial to inexperienced public speakers. One of the factors that makes public speaking such an anxiety-producing experience is fear of the unknown. If you are an inexperienced speaker, and you aren't sure what factors are important to your speech, then there is a good chance you will experience the fear of the unknown.

But following the guidance for doing specific types of speeches can take the edge off that fear and give you a bit of security in knowing that a given type of speech should have certain qualities and follow certain patterns. As you become a more experienced speaker, following the guidelines to a speech type might become less important. You might then be able to draw on your experience to guide your speeches as you mix the different aspects of various speech types just as an experienced cook can mix ingredients without following a strict recipe. But, as a beginner, working with specific speech types can be very helpful.

Selecting the Topic

Often when you learn that you will have to give a speech, the topic is already selected for you. Your supervisor may tell you that you will be asked to spend ten minutes at the next staff meeting outlining your department's goals for the coming quarter. Or your psychology instructor might ask students to explain a theory of behavior for an upcoming presentation. But other times, especially in classes beyond an introductory speech class, you will be expected to select your own topic, sometimes from a general set of possible topics or a general type of topic. When this happens, you should follow a clear topic-selection process that mirrors the process used by experienced writers and public speakers. This process involves *listing* potential topics and *asking questions* about those potential topics.

The steps in selecting a speech topic:

- Listing
- Asking questions

Listing: First you should list as many possible topics as you can within the general framework of the speech requirements. The type of speech you will be giving will help to focus your listing (see Section Four for details about types of speeches). If you are assigned an introduction speech in a history class where you must discuss a historical figure, jot down as many *people* from your history studies as you can think of. Or if you have to do a speech explaining a managerial style that you've studied in a business class, list potential management *subjects* and then potential related *objects* you can use in a "show-and-tell" speech about that concept. For a demonstration speech, list *processes* or *activities* that you might teach your audience how to do. For a persuasion speech, list *issues* that members of your audience might disagree about. For an impromptu speech (one in which you won't know the topic in advance), see if there is a way you can narrow down the potential topic range and make a list of *possible topics* to try to guess what topic you might have to speak about. And for a manuscript speech, list many possible *manuscripts* to read.

The most important part of listing is quantity— list as many possible topics as you can. Don't discard any topic because it might not seem worthwhile at first thought. Deciding which topic is best comes in the second step of topic selection: asking questions.

Asking Questions: When you have listed many potential topics, you can then discover which items from your list would make good topics by asking yourself these six simple yes/no questions about each potential topic:

1) Do I already know at least something about this topic? At least a basic knowledge about your topic is a good starting point when you begin preparing the content of your speech. You don't want to spend the bulk of your preparation time learning about the topic completely from scratch. For almost all speeches, in fact, the more you know about the topic you select, the better you can prepare for your speech.

2) Do I want to learn more about this topic? No matter how much you already know about the topic, one of the great facts of life is that you will continue to learn more by preparing a speech. So having an interest in the topic will make doing the speech more interesting than if you aren't interested in the topic.

3) Do I have enough preparation time to put together a speech on this topic? You will have certain practical constraints and deadlines that will make some topics too difficult for you to do your best preparation work.

4) Can I guess how my audience will react to this topic? You should address your speech to your audience as specifically as you can. You don't yet need to know exactly how your audience will respond, but it's wise to begin analyzing your audience early in the topic-selection stage to make the speech effective for that audience.

5) Can I cover this topic well within my speech time limit? You don't want to go under your time limit (a sign of being underprepared) or over your time limit (a sign of being disorganized or even egotistical). So pick a topic that fits your time limit. This is especially important for a demonstration speech where time often seems to stretch or shrink as you get into the particulars of demonstrating a process.

6) Am I clear about my attitude toward the topic? You will want to project a clear attitude about the topic to your audience, enhancing your authority and credibility, especially when doing persuasive speaking.

If your answers to these six questions about a potential topic are all yes, then you probably have a good topic for your speech. But if even one of the answers is no, that is a warning sign that it might not be a good topic, perhaps a topic that will ruin the speech even before you begin preparing it. If you have many topics with six yes responses, then you get to make a selection from many strong topics. Often consulting a trusted friend, colleague, classmate, or instructor can help you make the final selection. If you have no topics with six yes responses, then you should go back to the listing stage again to generate more potential topics.

As an inexperienced public speaker who might be taking a public speaking course, you should keep a special consideration in mind when you select a topic for your speech. You may be tempted to select a topic that is controversial because you hope it will get your audience's interest or because you believe very strongly in the topic.

Unfortunately, such topics are often very difficult, even for experienced public speakers. This is especially true when doing persuasion speeches. Topics such as capital punishment, abortion, welfare, gun control, religion, or smoking will certainly get your audience interested in your speech, but you will have an extremely difficult time doing a good job with such topics in a brief classroom speech. Experienced speakers such as members of Congress have trouble addressing these topics well in speeches that may run a full hour. Your much shorter practice speech in class will be a significantly better learning experience for you if you select an easier topic and invest your energies in the performance and content skills detailed later in this book.

Analyzing your Audience

Once you have a topic selected, you should try to find out a few things about your audience members. Who are they? You can investigate the audience's "demographics": their characteristics such as age, gender, and race, for example. Of course, not all people of the same age, gender or race think alike, but you can make some very general assumptions about your audience when you know these characteristics.

There are other questions you should ask about your audience. Why are they attending your speech? Will they be likely to share your view of the topic or not? For example, if you have to speak to a group of employees about cutbacks at your company, find out if this audience is among the people targeted for possible layoffs. That knowledge will certainly help shape the way you deliver your information.

If you can, survey your audience about their thoughts on your topic before your speech. (In a public speaking class, for example, you can take a show-of-hands poll about your topic a week or so before you give the speech, helping you to shape the content.) You can never learn all there is to know about your audience, but whatever you can find out will be useful to you as you prepare your speech.

Generating Information for the Speech

Once you have a workable topic, you should begin to develop the content of the speech, especially the main points and details.

The building blocks of speech content:

- Main points
- Details

The *main points* of a speech are the big ideas that you want to get across to your listeners, the ideas that will form the outline of your speech and that you will emphasize to your audience so that they will remember them after the speech is over. Freewriting, listing, and outside research (discussed below) can help you to discover your main points. If you are asked to discuss the most important qualities of a good worker at a business meeting, for example, you should list as many of those qualities as you can think of. Then you could select the most important ones to form the framework of the speech.

To develop the main points, you will also need *details*. Details are the specific bits of information that illustrate and support your main points. If one of your main points about the qualities of a good worker is that a good worker interacts well with colleagues, then you need to describe some specific examples of a good worker cooperating with coworkers to develop this point. Details can take many forms: facts, statistics, quotations from authorities, brief stories, scenarios, cases—as long as the details relate directly to the main point that they are illustrating. You can use freewriting, listing, and outside research to generate details, too.

Three methods of generating information for your speech:

- Freewriting
- Listing
- Exploring outside sources

We all have a vast treasure of experience and knowledge that can be used in a speech. Unfortunately, that treasure is locked up inside one of the most well-guarded fortresses ever created: our own minds. Public speakers (and writers) often have a great deal of trouble accessing the information in their own minds for lots of reasons (poor experiences with speaking and writing in school, lack of self-confidence, a learning disability, limited formal educational experience, a lack of practice with complex critical thinking skills, etc.). But two proven attention-focusing techniques can help to tap the information treasures of the mind: freewriting and listing. In addition, you can draw on other treasures of information beyond your own experience in the form of outside resources.

Freewriting: Freewriting is a strategy often used by writers, but it is equally applicable to generating information for public speaking. Freewriting is simply writing whatever pops into your mind as fast as you can without worrying about what the writing looks like or if it makes any sense. This is private writing that you don't have to share with anyone, so you are freed from the anxiety associated with other people judging your writing harshly. Of course, the freewriting won't make much sense when you first read it, and it's certainly not the kind of final wording that you would want to say in a speech. But the text generated through freewriting is great raw material that contains some terrific nuggets that can later be shaped into coherent information for your speech.

For example, suppose you are giving a speech about volcanoes. You might not be an expert on volcanoes, but you probably do have some personal knowledge about them that could become an important element of your speech. So you spend five minutes focusing your mind on volcanoes and writing down whatever pops into your head as fast as you can. (If nothing comes to mind right away, just write, "I can't think of anything" or "volcanoes" over and over until something does come to mind. This strategy might feel silly, but that's okay because it will naturally pull more useful information from your brain.) Perhaps you might jot down some phrases about the first time you saw a volcano on television when you were a child, noting how scared you were of the hot lava. Perhaps you were even worried about the hill next to your house erupting into a volcano. This freewritten material could eventually be shaped into an interesting transition in your speech where you talk about the causes of volcanoes and the fact that not every hill can simply erupt into a volcano. Your personal experience from childhood can form a moment in the speech that might connect with your listeners' experiences, creating a connection with your audience. The best method to discover information like this is through freewriting.

Listing: Listing is very similar to freewriting, but instead of writing from left to right in paragraph form, you write down the page in a list. The same principles of private writing that work in freewriting apply to listing. Don't worry about how others will judge your list because it is just for your own use.

One example of how listing can be useful for tapping the information in your mind might be a speech about why people should give money to charity. You could focus your mind on the reasons why giving to charity is a good thing, then list those reasons as they pop into your mind. Perhaps in three minutes of listing you come up with ten reasons. You might pick out the best four, combine another two reasons into one, and then discard the other four as not important. You would then have five reasons why giving money to charity is important. This could be the basis for an outline of your speech, completely generated through listing.

Exploring outside sources: There are many traditional outside sources that public speakers can tap to find information for their speeches. These sources include "library materials" (books, newspapers, magazines, and computerized indices and/or databases). The Internet, of course, is a vast outside source that is easily accessible to many people, although it contains both reliable and unreliable materials. For example, a blog written by someone who believes the debunked theory that President Obama was not born in the United States is a terrible source for reliable information about anything related to government. A ".gov" or ".edu" source would be far more reliable on that subject.

Information for speeches can also come from interviews with experts on the subject (in person, by telephone, e-mail, or letters). Finally, on-site resources such as memos, brochures, flyers, letters, and manuals that are related to your speech topics are often available at organization offices or companies. (There are many useful guidebooks about how to find information from outside sources, so this book will not focus on that aspect of preparing a speech).

If you find that you have gaps in your speech as you are generating material, there is no rule against going back and doing more freewriting, listing, or investigating outside sources. In fact, you will be well served by continuing these activities throughout the process of preparing your speech.

An important consideration to keep in mind concerning outside sources is that you don't need to know everything about libraries to find a library book or be an Internet expert to search for on-line information. You are not completely on your own. Every source of outside information that you might need to consult for your speeches has experts who can help you find what you need. Libraries have librarians who are professional information-finders and can provide excellent help in discovering everything from books to websites. Companies have public relations and information employees to send you materials. One of the keys to finding outside information is learning how to work with people who are there to help you.

When you use an outside source in a speech, you don't need to recite the type of bibliographic information that you would include on the last page of a documented research paper. The best way to document that source is to say something as simple as this: "According to Wendy Roberts, a psychologist and author of the book, *Twenty Nightmares*, the most common nightmare is one where we dream we are falling." If a great deal of your speech comes from one or two sources, acknowledge those sources early in the speech: "The statistics that I'll be presenting come from an article by Ken Williams that was published in *USA Today* on June 13, 2013." And if you distribute a handout or use visual aids when you give your speech, that's a good place to provide a written list of your sources. (Note: It's always good to have the *specific* source of the material handy in case someone asks you for it after the speech. If you can't cite your source when asked, your audience might doubt your credibility.)

Organizing the Speech

Once you have generated main points and details, you should begin to construct an outline of your speech. A fancy term for outlining a speech is developing a "rhetorical structure"—that is, an organization that best communicates the content of your speech. Most speeches done by native speakers of English follow a three-part, introduction-body-conclusion structure. Speakers from cultures where English is not the native language sometimes use rhetorical structures different from the one presented below. Asian cultures, for example, often use a "circular" rhetorical structure that gets to the main points less directly than the usual English-language structures. This is not to say that every Asian person communicates like every other Asian person—only that there are general cultural expectations that come into play during the communication process. In the United States, the general cultural expectation is an introduction-body-conclusion structure.

Also, no one specific way of structuring a speech is superior to any other; some structures are simply more appropriate for audiences whose cultural background shapes their expectations about how a speech will be structured. (In practical terms, if you plan to give speeches to audiences from a culture other than your own, you would benefit greatly from exploring the general rhetorical structures common to that culture.)

The rhetorical structure presented here is geared primarily for speakers and audiences whose native language is English. You may also have seen structures similar to the one presented below used for organizing essays in a writing class because this structure is very common to both written and verbal communication in cultures where English is the native language.

The basic structure of a speech:

- Introduction
- Body
- Conclusion

The *introduction* is a brief section at the beginning that prepares the audience for the body part of a speech. A speaker's introduction needs to serves these functions:

Capture the audience's interest: Open the speech with a "grabber," a strong statement that gets your audience's attention. For specific advice, see the guidelines on grabbers later in this section.

Provide needed background information about the topic: Give any essential information that the audience will need to know in order to understand the topic—for example, historical background or definitions of key terms. Background information of this sort will help to ensure that your audience is not confused by subsequent information as you go along with the speech.

Establish the central theme of the speech: Reveal the primary focus and/or purpose of the speech. Your central theme may not be perfectly clear to you as you are preparing the speech, but it should develop and reveal itself as you get further into your preparation. The central theme of an introduction speech, for instance, could be something as simple as "Jimmy Carter was a better president than he gets credit for being," or, for a demonstration speech, "Jump-starting a car battery is safe and easy if you know the proper procedure." Having a central theme serves two important purposes: First, it gives your audience members a focal point to come back to if they find their minds drifting during the speech; and second, it gives you, the speaker, a focal point to come back to if you find yourself moving off on unnecessary tangents as you prepare, organize, and deliver your speech.

Preview the main points of the speech: Provide your audience with a "roadmap" of the speech by naming or summarizing the main points to be covered in the body of the speech. For example, in a speech explaining public speaking anxiety, "There are four main types of fear associated with public speaking that I will explore today: fear of being the center of attention; fear of the unknown; fear of failure; and fear of rejection." Previewing your main points takes away some of the mystery to a speech, allowing your audience to know the direction your speech will take, making it easier for them to process the content as the body of the speech unfolds. If your speech has many main points, you don't need to number off all of those points in an awkward-sounding and time-consuming list. You can instead summarize those points into a clearer and more concise list.

The *body* is the largest part of a speech where the most important ideas are conveyed. The speaker serves these functions in the speech body:

Use transitions to guide the audience through the main points: Use simple phrases that let your audience know you are moving to a main point of the speech. Here are some examples of transitional phrases used to connect main points: "The *first* fear of public speaking is…"

"*Related to* the fear of failure is ..." "The *fourth* and *most important* reason why Jimmy Carter was a better president than he is given credit for being is ..." These transitions are statements that give important signals to your audience to show when you are moving from one point of emphasis to another. They allow your audience to process the information presented in the previous section, then focus on the point you are making in the upcoming section. Your audience can follow and remember the points of your speech much better when you use transitions effectively.

Provide the main points of the speech: State simply and clearly each particular main point, emphasize it vocally so that the audience remembers it, pause before and after it so it stands out, and repeat or restate it if necessary for further emphasis and clarification. Main points provide the framework for the bulk of a speech and are the most important general ideas that you want your audience to remember about your topic. Without clearly stated and emphasized main points, your audience might find your speech to be rambling and difficult to follow or remember—much like an essay with poor paragraphing. If you provide a handout to your audience or use an overhead projector or presentation software, your main points should be prominently displayed to help your audience follow the flow of the speech and remember the important ideas. Too few main points could make a speech too short, just as too many might make it too long.

Provide details to develop those main points: Flesh out each main point with specific examples, facts, statistics, illustrations, anecdotes, demonstrations, etc., so the audience can fully appreciate and understand each point. These details are the raw material that gives a speech depth and dimension. Inadequate details that don't fully illustrate your main points will leave your audience with incomplete knowledge, while inappropriate details that don't connect with your main points will leave your audience confused about the overall content of your speech. Similar to main points, not enough details can cause the speech to fall short of the time limit, and too many details can send a speech over the time limit.

The *conclusion* is a brief section at the end that ties a speech together clearly and completely. The speech's conclusion serves these functions:

Provide a transition to signal that the speech is nearing its end: Saying something as simple as "in conclusion," or "to sum up what we've covered," or "let's put this all together," will signal the audience that the main points have been covered and the speech will conclude shortly. When audience members get this transition signal, they will turn up the intensity of their attention because they know subconsciously the conclusion of a speech will contain important information. (They will also know that they only have to focus their attention for a short time until the speech is over, so this transition may sometimes lead to a collective audience sigh of relief is the speech is long.)

Review the central theme of the speech: Re-emphasize the central theme that was stated in the introduction and runs under the surface of the entire speech. In a very real sense, everything said during the speech should somehow relate to your central theme, so coming back to that theme near the end of the speech will make it even clearer for your audience.

Review the main points: Restate or summarize and

emphasize the main points first mentioned in the introduction and covered in the body of the speech so that the audience has the best chance possible of understanding and remembering them. Reviewing the main points just before closing the speech is essential because it takes advantage of the heightened attention the audience gives when it knows a speech is about to end. Remember to avoid simply repeating your main points or restating them as if the audience has never heard them before. Reviewing is the process of reminding your audience of the points you've made central to the organization of the speech.

Provide closure: Finish the speech with a strong "closer," tying the speech together and giving it a sense of completeness. For details about closers, see the guidelines on closers later in this section.

Give the "last words": Every speech should end with a sincere "thank you" to the audience for their attention. In addition, if there is time for questions, you should ask something like, "Are there any questions?" or state, "I can address your questions at this point."

If you are unsure how to structure your speech once you have generated information for the content, the introduction-body-conclusion structure is a very good place to start. As you develop more confidence in organizing your speeches, you can experiment with this structure and adapt it to your own personal public speaking style and needs. Section Four of this book shows how this general speech structure can be used with specific types of speeches.

Structure, repetition, and memory: At first glance, this general speech structure might seem unnecessarily repetitive, especially considering that the main points of the speech are previewed in the introduction, developed in the body, reviewed in the conclusion, and perhaps numbered as a transition. You might wonder whether or not audiences would start to think that you are addressing them as if they were children who needed everything repeated and numbered. This kind of repetition might feel somewhat boring to you as the speaker, but that's because you are so familiar with the content of your speech from having worked so hard to generate and organize it. Your *audience*, however, will not be so familiar with the speech's content as you are, and they won't be bored with you repeating and numbering your main points. Actually, most members of your audience will thank you for doing so because they will be able to process and remember your information more easily.

If you say the main points only once, the audience will have a hard time remembering them from one minute to the next, let alone hours, days, and weeks after the speech is over. But repeating the main points will help the audience retain them and will be especially useful if the audience members are taking notes on your speech because they can check to make sure they have written things down accurately. And using numbers as transitions between your main points will help your audience members keep their thoughts about your speech organized.

Think of teachers who are the hardest to follow in class or the bosses that rush through important information at meetings. They are usually the ones who *never* repeat big ideas unless you raise your hand to ask them to. Also, *this book itself* uses a repetitive structure similar to the one described here—and not because the author thinks you are stupid! Far from it. Hopefully, the structure will make it easier for you to read, remember, and put the book's content to use.

How structure can help you lengthen or shorten your speech: The length of a speech should be planned in accordance with the time limit allotted. Keeping to prescribed time limits is essential in connecting with your audience. If your speech is too short, your audience will think that you are unprepared or unknowledgeable about your subject—or just too lazy to put in the effort. And if your speech is well over the time limit, your audience will think that you are disorganized, a poor planner, or an arrogant jerk who thinks your time is more valuable than the audience members' time. In addition, if you are one of several speakers in a longer program, and your speech is over the time limit, an entire day's program might be thrown out of whack. So try to plan your speech so it fits as close as possible to your time limit.

The general introduction-body-conclusion speech structure can also help you lengthen or shorten a speech to fit a specific time limit.

To lengthen a speech:

- Add or subdivide main points
- Extend or add details

To shorten a speech:

- Delete or combine main points
- Condense or delete details

Here is an example of how main points and details can help you lengthen or shorten a speech: You might give a speech to your college class about the importance of fire safety in the home. The speech could be five minutes long (not including questions at the end) with a 30 second introduction and a 30 second conclusion and four main points with one minute of detail for each main point. Someone in your class might be very impressed with your speech and ask you to be a guest speaker at her monthly apartment building tenants' meeting. But for this meeting, you will have 20 minutes to speak on the topic of fire safety. How can you lengthen the speech without simply talking slowly and adding 15 minutes of pauses, umms, ahhs, and questions that you hope the audience will ask?

The two best methods for lengthening the speech are adding main points and/or adding details. You could go back to your original notes when you were first developing the speech and discover four more main points that were interesting but not essential enough for the five-minute version of the speech. Because you now have much more time and an audience especially interested in information about your topic, you can work these four points into the speech. You can also add another minute of details to the original four main points so that these each point now have two minutes of details, then generate two minutes of details for each of the four new main points. You now have eight main points with two minutes of details each, a minute for your introduction, another minute for your conclusion, and an extra few minutes in reserve for questions after the speech. (Note: Even when a speech gets much longer, the introduction and conclusion usually remain relatively brief.)

Shortening a speech works exactly the same way—but in reverse. You can delete or combine main points and/or delete or condense details.

Grabbers and closers: Introductions and conclusions are especially important moments in any speech, so they deserve special attention. Audience members remember the beginning and end of a speech more than the middle. There are no worse ways of beginning a speech than by saying, "My speech is about…" or "Today I will be speaking on the topic…" or even, "Hi. How is everyone today?" These openings will send your audience directly to sleepy-land and may even undermine your credibility right from the start of your speech. In the same way, ending a speech weakly by saying, "That's it. I'm done…" or "That's about all I have to say, I guess…" does nothing more than signal your audience to wake up and perhaps applaud out of polite pity.

Good speeches should begin and end strongly. That's where you need "grabbers" and "closers." These are ways of opening your speech that grab the audience's attention and ending the speech with a sense of closure that pulls the speech together for the audience. Grabbers and closers must be delivered with enthusiasm, energy, and authority to give them the kind of emphasis that will make your audience take notice. Generating enthusiasm and authority can sometimes be difficult—especially delivering a grabber at the beginning of your speech, just at the moment when you are probably most anxious. But you need to turn that anxiety into energy and deliver the grabber strongly to start the speech with a bang.

41

Grabber techniques to open your speech on a strong note:

Ask a question: Ask, "How many of you ever broke a bone playing a sport as a child or teenager?" at the beginning of a speech about safety in children's sports. Be sure to give your audience time to respond to the question with a show of hands or a couple of comments. And be sure to express your genuine interest in their responses.

Use a prop: Show a cute paper ladybug design before a demonstration speech showing how these ladybugs can be made quickly and easily with just a few supplies. Be sure to hold the prop up so that the audience can see it clearly for at least a few seconds and to pass it around the room if appropriate.

Make a dramatic or surprising statement: Say, "Every 17 seconds, someone in the United States is killed with a firearm" to open a speech about responsible gun ownership. Be sure to pause after the statement and repeat it for emphasis so the full effect can sink in with your audience.

Tell a brief story: Open a speech about the value of high school music programs by telling about the thrill of the first time you played the flute in a school recital. These brief stories are often called anecdotes, and they can be strong methods for establishing a personal connection with your audience members. Be sure that you connect the story with the central theme of your speech so as not to confuse your audience. Also, if you have a relatively short speech, be sure to keep the opening anecdote correspondingly brief as well.

Use a quotation: To open a speech about Martin Luther King or the Civil Rights Movement, quote a few stirring lines from King's writings or speeches. Be sure to introduce the quotation clearly, if necessary, to mention where the quote comes from, and to connect the quotes with your overall topic.

Use a statistic: For a speech about recycling, give the exact number of pounds of garbage discarded every day and the exact cost of processing that garbage. Be sure to use a statistic that will be clear to your audience and to mention the source of the statistic.

Use humor: For a speech about ways to deal with stress, begin with a humorous account of the stress associated with your preparation for the speech. Gentle, self-directed humor is usually best for getting the audience on your side right from the beginning of the speech. Remember that jokes or humor directed at anyone other than yourself run the risk of offending your audience, so make your humor respectful rather than disparaging.

Make a call to action: At the beginning of a speech about adopting a new sales philosophy for your company, tell your audience that they will be able to double their commissions if they listen closely to your speech.

Closer techniques to conclude your speech on a strong note (follow these with the standard, "Thank you," and invite questions, if there is time):

Ask a question: Ask, "*Now* how do you feel about casino gambling?" after a speech about its negative effects of casinos on a community.

Use a prop: Tear a dollar bill in half to conclude a speech about the taxpayer money spent on the Iraq and Afghanistan wars.

Make a dramatic or surprising statement: After a speech explaining the importance of a specific battle in World War II, inform your audience that you became interested in this subject because your grandfather fought in that battle.

Tell a brief story: Conclude a speech about how to make the world's greatest chocolate cake by telling the story of how even your crabby uncle learned to love you because you made one of these cakes for his birthday.

Use a quotation: To conclude a speech about the stress of driving, quote from James Taylor's classic song, "Traffic Jam."

Use a statistic: For a speech about mental illness, re-emphasize the percentage of people in the United States with some form of mental illness, and then use that statistic to estimate how many people in the audience suffer from mental illness (without, of course, naming or pointing toward any audience members!).

Use humor: To conclude a speech about why owning a small economy car is the best option for a college student, tell the people in your audience that you can't offer them rides home because your car is too small—but present this as an advantage.

Make a call to action: At the end of a speech about a political candidate, encourage the audience not just to vote for that candidate, but to work on his or her campaign as well.

Framing the grabber and closer: A final strategy for making good grabbers and closers is called framing. This involves ending the speech by connecting back to the beginning. For example, you might repeat or restate the same surprising statement at the end that you presented at the beginning. Or you might ask the same question for a closer that you did as your grabber—but now the audience can answer the question with more certainty because they have the knowledge that you've given them in the speech. Framing works well to tie the speech together for the audience, giving them a sense that they have heard a coherent, whole speech rather than just a series of unrelated statements.

Practicing the Speech

As the time for your speech approaches, you should move from preparing the *content* of the speech (topic, organization, details, etc.) to practicing the *performance* the speech. (The essential concepts of "content" and "performance" are covered in detail later in this book.) This practice involves as much rehearsal as possible.

When you have your speaking notes prepared (an example of speaking notes is included later in this section), you should practice delivering the speech as if you were actually performing it for your audience. Practice the speech alone at home when you are doing routine activities. Or lock yourself in the bathroom away from your family where you can concentrate on practicing the speech while watching yourself in the mirror. Then find some people whom you can trust (co-workers, classmates, friends, family members) and practice the speech in front of them, asking them for constructive feedback on your performance. Focus on projecting your voice and speaking clearly, visualizing eye-contact with audience members, gesturing naturally and relaxing your body language, and investing the speech with energy and authority. (Section Three provides details on specific guidance and practice activities to develop the performance aspects of your speech.)

As a practical consideration, be sure to scout the location before you actually give the speech, even a few days in advance if possible. Get a feel for where you will be standing, where the audience will be, and how you can use the room to help you connect with your audience. If you can arrange to do so, you should try to practice the speech a few times in the room where you will actually present it to your audience.

All this practice may seem awkward or even obsessive, but the more you are able to work through the kinks of the speech and be comfortable with presenting the content through a strong performance, the better the speech is likely to go when you are actually faced with your real audience.

Evaluating the developing speech: As you practice the speech, you should also assess how well your speech matches the qualities that make your type of speech successful. These qualities are detailed in Section Four and should be used as touchstones, revisited again and again to help you judge whether or not your speech will be as effective as possible. You need to be willing to revise your speech as you prepare it so that it will correspond to these qualities as closely as possible.

For example, if you discover your demonstration speech takes too much time describing the tools, supplies, and time needed and not enough on the process being demonstrated, then you will need to revise your speech to balance this information. Or if your persuasion speech is coming down too hard on audience members who may disagree with your position, you need to revise the speech to make your tone more respectful. It's useful to photocopy or write down the qualities of an effective speech of the type you are preparing and keep that list with you and refer to it often when practicing your speech.

Visualizing yourself delivering the speech well: If you have prepared and practiced your speech, you should feel more confident when the actual moment arrives. When you are waiting for your name to be called in class before a presentation or waiting for your item of the agenda at a work meeting, review your notes one final time, just to be sure of your main points. Even more important, you should use these moments to visualize yourself at the podium doing a good job with the speech. Picture yourself projecting your voice, making eye-contact with your audience, gesturing expressively, and putting energy and authority into the speech. In short, picture yourself succeeding—that will increase your chance of succeeding when you actually begin the speech.

Section Three:
How to Give a Speech

Actually giving a speech involves many things: effective performance and content, making speaking notes, providing handouts for your audience, and focusing your thinking during the speech.

The two most important aspects of giving a speech:

- Performance
- Content

Strong public speaking involves mastering two specific, separate, interrelated skills: *performance* and *content*. Performance skills involve presenting yourself to an audience in an effective way, while content skills involve presenting *information* to your audience in a clear way. Content is developed as you "write" the speech; performance is demonstrated as you "deliver" the speech. You have the best chance to improve yourself as a public speaker if you think of these two skills as separate units and develop them separately, then unite them in the presentation of a speech. As you develop one aspect, the other tends to improve as well. For example, when you are less anxious about your public speaking performance, you can focus your energies on generating the content of your speech. Or when you are confident about the content of your speech, you can work on performing well when you present that content.

A good way to think about performance and content is to break each aspect into its component parts.

The four major components of public speaking performance:

- Voice
- Eye-contact
- Body language
- "Personality" put into a speech

The four major components of public speaking content:

- Introduction
- Organization
- Development
- Conclusion

Performance

The following sections elaborate on the four components of public speaking *performance* and describe different levels of execution for each of these components, from outstanding (A) to failing (F).

Voice: Voice is the primary tool of any public speaker. On the surface, your voice is what conveys the content of your speech through your words. But in a deeper way, your voice can help you connect with an audience. Strong public speaking involves projecting, controlling, and pacing your voice so that you can be heard and understood by the entire audience.

The first important element of voice is *volume*. Obviously, your audience must be able to hear what you're saying. A strong public speaking voice should be significantly louder than a one-on-one conversational voice. Because many speeches are given without benefit of a microphone, you need to increase the volume of your voice to be heard throughout whatever room you are speaking in. This means that your voice should be strong and clearly audible to audience members who are *farthest away* from you. The people in the *back* of the room are the ones you should use as a measure to judge the volume of your voice.

At times, you may feel as though you are shouting to your audience when you give your voice the strong volume that public speaking calls for. And you might worry that your audience will think you are a maniac who is yelling at them. Strong volume will only sound overly loud to you because your ears are a great deal closer to your mouth than the ears of your audience members (well, we should hope so!). Your audience will actually be grateful for your strong volume. Strong volume in your public speaking voice will allow you to "command" the room, helping to make effective listening easer for your audience during your speech.

Closely related to volume is *projection*. You need to push your voice out to the audience so that it carries. You should make sure you aren't projecting your voice down into your speaking notes, but out to your audience. Such projection can be very difficult if you find yourself relying too heavily on your speaking notes. But if you have prepared the content of your speech effectively, your voice should project well because you will only have to glance at your notes once in a while and can spend most of your speech looking at, and thus projecting your voice to, your audience. Also, some people are naturally prone to look up at the ceiling as they speak. This will inhibit the way your audience

---

hears your voice. If you have this tendency, practice projecting directly *out* to the audience, rather up to the ceiling.

If you have a *microphone* for your speech, however, voice considerations will be a bit different. You should check out the microphone before your actual speech if possible. All microphones are a little bit different; some should be only a few inches from your mouth, some up to two feet, some clipped, some held. If you can't test the microphone before the speech, assume that it should be at about your breast bone so that it doesn't hide your face from the audience. Simply grab the microphone once and adjust it to the proper height, and then start talking. Don't fiddle with the microphone during the speech because that will distract your audience from what you're saying and make you appear nervous. You still need to project your voice when speaking into a microphone to invest your performance with energy.

The pace of your voice is also important. Your voice should be paced like a CNN newscaster's—not too fast and not too slow. Fast talkers have a tendency to give out information so quickly that the audience can have trouble keeping up and processing the information presented. Listening to a fast talker is actually very hard work, tiring out an audience and making it difficult for them to pay attention. On the other hand, slow talkers also tire out an audience by boring them, "putting them to sleep" as people say. A middle ground between fast and slow is the best pace for public speaking.

This grading breakdown describes different levels of voice in a speech:

A) Very clear, very strong voice, heard everywhere in the room, commands attention through voice, very well paced.
B) Solid, steady voice, well projected, well paced, but could do more to command listeners' attention
C) Fairly clear voice, but sometimes hard to hear, some problems with pacing, doesn't really command listeners' attention
D) Weak voice, a strain for listeners to hear, poorly paced, did very little to command listeners' attention
F) Very weak voice, much of the speech not heard by listeners, major problems with pace, does nothing to command listeners' attention

Eye contact: Your whole audience will be looking at you during your speech, so, naturally, they expect you to look back at them—no matter how intimidating that sounds. Strong public speaking involves directly seeing your audience so that you can connect and communicate with them. If you don't look at your audience during your speech, they will unconsciously assume that you don't respect them or care about their opinion of you. This will quickly lead to distrust between audience and speaker.

Just as your voice needs to be heard throughout the room, your eye-contact also needs to touch every member of the audience. It's most natural to look at audience members in the front or middle of the room, but you need to make special efforts to see the people sitting in the back and sides of the room. The best way to accomplish full eye-contact with your audience is to scan your view slowly from person to person, one side of the room to the other, front and back, taking moments here and there to linger on specific faces that are looking at you with special intensity. (You might feel an urge to glance away from the audience members looking at you intently, but these are the people who will most welcome and expect your eye-contact—so give it to them in strong doses.)

In addition to seeing the whole audience, you need to maintain eye-contact through as much of the speech as possible. This is especially difficult for inexperienced public speakers because they tend to be most dependent on their speaking notes. But if you practice your speech enough in advance to be very familiar with your content, and if you have good speaking notes (like the examples provided later in this book that list your main points and important details), you should be able to avoid looking down at your notes for extended periods or glancing down too frequently. Looking down too much breaks the eye-contact connection with your audience and muffles your voice by sending it down to the podium instead of out to the audience.

Three pieces of eye-contact "advice" often given to inexperienced public speakers are actually very misguided:

Looking just above your audience members' heads: The assumption behind this piece of advice is that pretending to make eye-contact with your audience is just as good as actually making eye-contact. The major problem with this thinking is that you won't be able to see your audience and respond to their feedback. If they look bored, you won't be able to notice that fact and respond appropriately by spicing up the speech. Also, audiences are not unobservant; they will know when you are only pretending to make eye-contact, and they won't like it.

Finding one friendly looking face and looking only at that person: All speakers would like to make their speeches less anxiety-producing by making them similar to a one-on-one conversation. But if you look only at one person, the rest of your audience will feel neglected, perhaps on a conscious level, but certainly unconsciously. In addition, the person you focus on may become very nervous because of your "fatal attraction" attention.

Picturing your audience in their underwear or naked: The intended effect of this strategy is to make your audience seem less intimidating and therefore easier subjects for make eye-contact. However, most people actually find naked people quite intimidating. When was the last time you were able to make extensive eye-contact with a room full of naked people?

How does a *video camera* in the room recording your speech affect your eye-contact? If there is a video camera, you don't need to pay undue attention to it. Just treat it as another member of your audience, looking at it occasionally to establish a sense of eye-contact with the audience that might be viewing the video of your speech. If the camera is recording your speech for a large audience (for instance, a television broadcast), then treat the camera as a *very important* member of your audience, giving it special attention (although not to the exclusion of your live audience). The video audience will actually appreciate the attention you pay to the in-person audience and assume you are a comfortable and confident speaker if you make more eye-contact with real people than with the video camera.

If there is a photographer taking still photos during your speech, the strategy is somewhat different. You should completely ignore the person taking pictures. That may seem rude, but photographers expect to be ignored. The still photographer's job is to capture the speech in a "candid" way, as if he or she were not even there. You will be very tempted to stare at the photographer or call attention to the fact that your picture is being taken by saying something like, "I'm so nervous when my picture is being taken." But this adds nothing of substance to your speech and serves as an unwanted distraction. Just ignore the shutterbug as much as possible.

This grading breakdown describes different levels of eye-contact in a speech:

A) Excellent eye-contact, sees and connects with everyone in the room throughout the speech
B) Solid eye-contact, but doesn't quite see or connect with whole audience throughout the speech
C) Needs to see more of the audience more often to connect with listeners during the speech
D) Doesn't see much of the audience or make any connections through eye-contact during large portions of the speech
F) Doesn't see audience at all and makes no eye-contact connections with listeners during the speech

Body language: Audiences read a speaker's body language almost as clearly as they hear a speaker's words—and sometimes even more clearly. Strong public speaking involves using your body to connect with your audience and to help communicate and emphasize your message.

Your *gestures* should be relaxed and natural. Hand and arm gestures are the most obvious ones made by public speakers. These gestures should be in a "zone of gesturation" (a two-foot square in front of your face and chest) so that your audience can actually see them. Extending an open hand or holding up three fingers when you introduce your third main point can help you to express and emphasize important ideas so that your audience can recognize which points are most important. And these kinds of gestures can show the audience that you care about your topic enough that you are "moved" to move. Of course, you don't want to go to the extreme of pounding the podium every few seconds or waving your arms over your head like a maniac. Such behavior tends to distract the audience from the content of your speech rather than emphasize and amplify your content.

Posture also helps convey meaning to your audience, especially messages about who you are. A slouching posture suggests to the audience that you are lazy, sloppy, weak-willed, or disorganized. A stiff, overly erect posture suggests to the audience that you are rigid and intolerant of other points of view. Standing too still tells them that you are distant, while dancing from foot to foot tells the audience that you are nervous. The best posture is simply standing straight behind the podium and squarely facing your audience—relaxed but not slouching or dancing, confident but not rigid. Of course, as you get more comfortable being in front of an audience, feel free to venture out from behind the podium and "Oprah" with the crowd.

Your *facial expressions* also communicate a great deal to your audience. Knitting your eyebrows during an important point in your speech can emphasize that point strongly. And smiling at our audience at almost any point in the speech is very appropriate and powerful (sometimes even at moments that seem not to be ones to smile about—very serious or sad points, for example).

In fact, the smile is one of a public speaker's secret weapons for keeping an audience interested, alert, and comfortable. When you smile at your audience members, they are likely to smile back and appreciate the efforts you are putting forth to communicate with them. Your smile tells your audience, "We're in this together," and connects with them the same way a strong voice and good eye-contact does.

This grading breakdown describes different levels of body language in a speech:

A) Looks relaxed and moves very naturally and expressively
B) Mostly relaxed, natural, and expressive
C) Somewhat stiff and unnatural; should be more expressive
D) Mostly stiff and unnatural; needs to be much more expressive
F) Completely stiff, unnatural, and inexpressive

"Personality" put into the speech: A public speaker should not be anonymous or distant from his or her audience. You need to communicate who you are just as much as what you have to say. Strong public speaking involves investing your performance with appropriate energy, enthusiasm, and authority to reveal

yourself to your audience.

Being *energetic* and *enthusiastic* about your topic lets your audience members know that you care about them and you care about what you are saying. If you can't generate enthusiasm during your speech, the audience will naturally be prone to boredom. But energy is contagious; if you are energetic, then your audience is likely to be pulled along by your energy, regardless of how they might have felt about your topic or about you before the speech began. (There are no boring topics, the old saying goes, just boring speeches.)

Smiling and *laughing* at appropriate moments can enhance the personal elements that you bring to your speech. (Smiling is discussed as a component of body language above.) Laughing is another way to connect with your audience, as long as it's not laughter intended to be overly sarcastic or hurtful. You don't need to be a stand-up comedienne, but if you say something that is meant to be humorous, it's okay to laugh at your own joke (as long as you don't laugh harder or louder than your audience does!). Any humor you might bring to your speech can be enhanced by your own laughter. In fact, unless you are cultivating an exaggerated "dry" delivery technique, your audience may think you are a bit stiff if you do not at least chuckle at your own humor. (Don't be discouraged if your audience doesn't laugh along with you at every humorous moment— simply go on with the speech. Even the best comediennes aren't funny every time. The audience will probably respond better to the next light moment.)

Displaying *authority* tells your audience that you know your topic and are worth listening to when speaking about that topic. Much of your authority will come from the content of your speech, especially having clear main points that make sense and enough specific details to illustrate those main points. But authority also comes from the attitude you display at the podium. And much of that attitude comes from the interplay between other aspects of public speaking performance: voice, eye-contact, and body language. If you project your voice strongly, hold eye-contact with your whole audience, and enhance your words through appropriate gestures and expressions, you will project a clear sense of authority to your audience.

Your personality is also reflected in the *clothing* you wear for your speech. There are many useful books available on how to "dress for success," so that subject won't be explored in great detail here. If you are in a public speaking class, your teacher might establish a dress code for delivering speeches, but that is most commonly left up to the individual students in the class. In other classes and in the professional world, a good guideline to follow is to dress a bit better than you would dress if you were a member of the audience. When giving a presentation to the class, for example, your audience members might be dressed casually (jeans, t-shirts, etc.), so you should wear a skirt, dress, fairly nice shirt, and/or slacks. A business dress or suit would be a bit too much in this case and might make you appear "snooty." In a business situation, however, your audience might be wearing business clothes, so a dress or suit would be more appropriate and expected.

One specific rule related to dress should always be followed when giving a speech; do not wear sunglasses or a hat, unless you have a medical condition that makes these items necessary. The right pair of sunglasses may make a terrific fashion statement in many situations, and a hat may help on a bad-hair day, but during a speech, they block eye-contact and will give your audience the impression that you are overly casual, distant, or even arrogant.

This grading breakdown describes different levels of "personality" in a speech:

A) Lots of confidence and authority; enthusiasm and energy appropriate for the topic
B) Mostly confident, energetic, authoritative, and enthusiastic
C) Some confidence, energy, and authority, but should show more
D) Needs much more confidence, enthusiasm, authority, and personality
F) Nothing of yourself in the speech except anxiety or arrogance

Practice Activities for Improving your Public Speaking Performance

Just as practicing a sport, hobby, or job-related activity will make you better at doing that activity, practicing public speaking performance will make you a better public speaker. Of course, the best way to practice public speaking performance is to give speeches. But there are also many informal activities that you can do to develop specific aspects of public speaking performance so that you can do them well when you give a speech.

Some of these practice activities may seem a bit silly at first glance, but they can significantly improve your performance abilities, and many of them can be done in a public speaking class or on your own outside class. These activities are very much like the training a professional athlete does. For example, Maya Moore, basketball star for the Minnesota Lynx, spends a great deal of training time lifting weights and riding an exercise bicycle. When she is playing in a basketball game, however, she never has to life an iron bar above her head or pedal a bike up and down the court. But her weight and cycle training are exceptionally valuable when she has to push other players for rebounding position or sprint down court on a fast break. These practice activities work the same way; you will never have to do these exact behaviors when you give a speech, but you will be able to deliver a better speech with more performance skill if you do these activities.

Voice:

In class: Go to the podium in front of the room and simply count to 10 or 20 at a medium pace. Have the instructor or some classmates stand in the back of the room and point up if you need to talk louder or down if you need to talk softer. Then go to the back of the room and listen to your classmates and advise them on talking louder or softer as they count.

Outside class: Any activity that forces you to increase your volume and projection makes a useful practice activity to develop your public speaking voice. One way to get this kind of practice is to find a private place (bedroom, bathroom, closet, car—wherever) and talk as loudly as you can (not quite shouting). Recite the Pledge of Allegiance, read from the newspaper, speak the lyrics to a favorite song, or say anything that allows you to listen to your full public speaking voice. (Of course, you want to assure your privacy for this activity or other people might come knocking at the door to see whom you are arguing with!)

Another activity is to stand downstairs and talk to someone who is upstairs. Increase your volume and project your voice so the person upstairs can hear you clearly. Or go outside and talk with someone who is at a distance from you, perhaps down the street or across an athletic field. (Parents will already have some practice with these last two activities, speaking loudly enough to be heard by distracted children.)

The bottom line is that all of these activities give you the experience of talking louder and projecting your voice more than you do in everyday conversation. Once you have this experience, you should remember how it feels so that you can bring that voice to your actual speeches.

Eye-contact:

In class: Very early in your course, take turns with your classmates walking up to the podium and making eye-contact with your audience without saying anything. Simply get used to the idea of looking at you audience from the front of the room. See where all the audience members are, what they look like, and how it feels to have them looking back at you. (You might feel like giggling or saying something to break the tension, and that's okay.) Do this for as short as 10 seconds or as long as a minute.

This can be an intimidating activity, but it's much better to see what your audience looks like in an ungraded practice session such as this than to see them for the first time when you go up to deliver your first speech. The view from the front of the room with so many sets of eyes looking back at you is much different from the view you are used to sitting in your chair in the classroom. This practice activity should take away some of the pressure of eye-contact from your early speeches.

An added benefit of this activity is that your audience gets a chance to look at you as you stand at the podium. We all have personal concerns about our bodies, faces, hair, and other aspects of our appearance, so it's much better to begin getting some of these concerns out of the way before giving your first speech, when you will have enough general public speaking concerns to worry about.

Outside class: Your own mirror is a great public speaking tool; use it to develop your ability to maintain eye-contact by practicing looking at yourself as you rehearse a speech. Start off with just one mirror and concentrate on holding eye-contact with yourself without looking at your speaking notes very often. Then, if you have the space, set up three or four mirrors around the sides and middle of the room that reflect back to you. Then practice making eye-contact with yourself in various locations throughout the room.

Looking in a mirror may seem like a silly way to practice speaking, but if you can use it to brush your teeth and comb your hair, you can use it to practice making eye-contact!

Another activity that will give you practice with eye-contact is monitoring your eye-contact in one-on-one conversations. See how often you look at a person you are having a conversation with, how often that person looks at you, and how long you hold eye-contact with that person. Try to hold eye-contact longer than you usually do in conversations so that you get more and more used to the feel of maintaining eye-contact in non-threatening situations like speaking one-on-one with a friend. It may seem cliché, but practicing one-on-one eye-contact will help your public speaking because making a speech to an audience is simply speaking one-on-one-and-one-and-one-and-one-and-one, etc.

Body language:

In class: Body language is especially important when doing demonstration speeches because you are doing something with your body (usually focused on using your hands) while talking and maintaining eye-contact with your audience.

An activity that can help you develop good demonstration body language is to go to the front of the room and tear sheets of paper into strips while telling the audience how you are doing it and making eye-contact with your audience. The trick is to be so used to the process you are demonstrating that you don't have to look while doing it or think about it too much and can instead keep talking to and looking at your audience. For variety, this activity can be done with any simple process; instead of tearing paper, for example, turning the pages of a book, pouring glasses of water, or unwrapping individually wrapped pieces of candy. (Tearing paper is a favorite, however, because it lets you take out a few frustrations!)

Outside class: Every person has his or her own natural set of gestures that he or she uses in everyday speaking situations. To find your own natural gestures, pay attention your normal conversations to see what you do with your hands. Discover your favorite gestures that help you emphasize important points and practice those gestures to make them as effective as possible when you use them in your speeches.

You can also speak to a mirror or videotape yourself and watch your gestures, posture, facial expressions, and overall body movements, practicing emphasizing positive body language that helps to communicate the content of our speech. If you seem to be too expressive to the point where your body language distracts from the content of your speech, you can work on toning down your body language. This may sound a bit like "acting" practice, but that's okay because there is an element of acting in effective public speaking performance. In a sense, everyone can teach himself or herself to become a more effective public speaking performer.

"Personality" put into the speech:

In class: Because the "personality" a speaker puts into a speech is often the element that works best to keep the audience focused and connected with the speaker, speaking to a distracted audience can be productive. For this activity, each person should go to the podium and count to 10 or 20 while the audience murmurs over and over the phrases "peas and carrots" and "rutabaga rhubarb." (These are the phrases actors say to mimic crowd noise in moves or TV shows when, for example, the jury announces a surprising verdict at the end of a dramatic trial.)

The murmuring of the audience will effectively simulate a very distracted audience. The only way that a speaker can communicate with an audience this distracted is to bring lots of personality to the speech.

In this practice activity, you will need to count your numbers with great energy, enthusiasm, and authority. If you can get through to a practice audience that is busy mumbling nonsense phrases like these, then you should be able to win over a real audience that might be a bit distracted because they are at the end of a long work day or seem not to be interested in the topic you are speaking about.

Outside class: The smile is a great advantage to a public speaker, so for this activity, once again get out your mirror or video camera and practice smiling as you talk. (Combining smiling and talking is more difficult than it might seem because your mouth is trying to do two things at once!) The more practice you can put into your public speaking smile, the more effective it will be when you get up in front of your audience.

Another way to monitor the "personality" you bring to your speeches is to videotape yourself giving a speech, and then turn the sound off as you watch the videotape. Without the distraction of hearing your words, you will be able to analyze how much energy, enthusiasm, and authority is coming through during your speech. If you see elements of personality that you like on the videotape, note them and practice bringing them to your future speeches. If you see elements that bother you, practice eliminating them from your future speeches.

You can also watch speeches on television with the sound off to evaluate the character of the people doing the speaking. This can be an especially effective way to assess politicians. Turn your TV to C-SPAN with the sound off and see if the members of our federal government look energetic, enthusiastic, and authoritative as they give the speeches we elected them to give. (Then keep this analysis in mind the next time you step into the voting booth!)

Common Performance Problems that Will Turn Off your Audience

All public speakers are at least a little bit nervous about doing something that might make the audience not like them. Audiences generally want to like public speakers, but certain behaviors (many of which speakers don't even know that they're doing) can turn off an audience. If you know you have any of these or similar behaviors, or if you observe them in yourself when you watch a video of your speeches, you should work to avoid them to keep the audience on your side.

Voice:

- speaking before the audience is ready to listen
- talking too loudly or softly, too fast or too slowly
- projecting your voice down into your notes instead of out to the audience
- using verbalized pauses such as "umm," "ya know," "okay," "so," or "like" too often

Eye-contact:

- looking only down the middle of the audience without looking at the people on both sides
- staring at only one place throughout the speech
- looking at only the teacher or boss

- looking down at the podium throughout the speech
- looking over the audience members' heads
- wearing sunglasses or a hat that shadows your eyes

Body language:

- tapping the podium or drumming your fingers
- shifting your weight back and forth too much
- gesturing too much or not at all
- not bringing your gestures up to your chest and face in the "zone of gesturation"
- gesturing frantically
- keeping your hands in your pockets
- leaning over the podium too far, slouching, or standing rigidly straight
- playing with your clothes, hair, face, or jewelry
- jingling coins or keys
- wringing or shaking your hands
- glancing at your watch or the clock too obviously
- cracking your knuckles

"Personality" put into the speech:

- walking to the podium like a child about to be punished
- apologizing for being nervous
- panicking if the speech isn't going as well as you had hoped
- appearing overly arrogant or overly self-conscious

- laughing harshly, at inappropriate times, or not at all
- reading too closely from a manuscript or relying too much on your notes
- not smiling at appropriate moments
- dressing inappropriately for the occasion
- running from the podium at the end of the speech

Content

The following sections elaborate on the four components of public speaking *content* and describe different levels of execution for each of these components, from outstanding (A) to failing (F). (For a complete understanding of public speaking content, see also the information on organizing a speech presented in Section Two.)

Introduction: Strong public speaking involves providing an introduction that draws your audience in and provides a roadmap to help them follow the speech.

This grading breakdown describes different levels of an introduction to a speech:

A) Enthralls audience, introduces central idea clearly, provides excellent background information, and previews main points clearly
B) Grabs audience's attention well, introduces central idea well, provides strong background information, and previews main points

C) Gets audience's attention adequately, introduces central idea fairly well, provides some background information, and names main points
D) Doesn't get audience's attention, introduces central idea poorly, provides inappropriate background information, and doesn't preview main points
F) Bores audience, makes central idea confusing, provides no background information, and ignores or confuses main points

Organization: Strong public speaking involves presenting information in a logical, well-emphasized sequence of main points that your audience can follow and remember.

This grading breakdown describes different levels of organization in a speech:

A) Main points are very clearly stated, very well ordered, and very well emphasized
B) Main points are clearly stated, well ordered, and well emphasized
C) Main points are fairly clearly stated and ordered and adequately emphasized
D) Main points are confusing, poorly ordered, and not well emphasized
F) Rambling, no main points

Development: Strong public speaking involves providing appropriate specific examples and details to illustrate, clarify, and/or support your main points.

This grading breakdown describes different levels of development in a speech:

A) Main points are very well developed with many appropriate specific examples and details
B) Main points are mostly well developed with appropriate specific examples and details
C) Main points are adequately developed with some appropriate specific examples and details
D) Main points are not well developed with only a few or vague examples and details
F) Main points are underdeveloped with no or very unclear examples and details

Conclusion: Strong public speaking involves ending the speech in a way that re-emphasizes the central idea, reviews the main points, and provides a sense of closure.

This grading breakdown describes different levels of a conclusion to a speech:

A) Re-emphasizes central idea clearly, reviews main points very well, and has a powerful closer
B) Re-emphasizes central idea clearly, reviews main points well, and has a strong closer
C) Re-emphasizes central idea adequately, restates main points, and has an adequate closer
D) Doesn't re-emphasize central idea or review main points well, and has a weak closer
F) Fades to an end or seems to be cut off in mid-thought as a speaker springs from the podium

Common Content Problems
that Will Confuse your Audience

Keeping the content of your speech as clear as possible is important for making sure that your audience can understand and remember what you are saying. Some easily avoided content errors can hurt your speech. As you prepare your speech, look to eliminate problems such as these to help your audience follow the content clearly.

Introduction:

- saying, "Hi, how is everybody?" at the beginning of the speech instead of starting with a strong grabber
- saying something like, "my speech is about" at the beginning of the speech instead of starting with a strong grabber
- saying your grabber before your audience is ready to listen
- not emphasizing your grabber strongly enough to give it impact
- opening with a question but not giving your audience time to consider it
- not indicating the central idea of the speech
- neglecting to preview your main points of the speech
- having an overly long introduction that takes attention away from the body of the speech and puts the speech over the time limit

Organization:

- not using transitions to lead from one main point to the next
- failing to vocally emphasize your main points strongly enough
- failing to pause as a way to emphasize your main points
- calling your main points "things" instead of clearly connecting them with your central theme
- outlining the speech in an illogical sequence of main points
- rambling without any main points at all
- failing to provide a handout that lists the main points of the speech
- having too few main points that results in the speech being under the time limit
- having too many main points that results in the speech being over the time limit

Development:

- not having enough specific examples and details to illustrate your main points
- having too many specifics to develop some main points but not enough for others
- rushing through the presentation of specific examples and details
- using specifics that don't relate to the main point you are making
- using complex specifics without explaining them so that your audience will understand
- failing to define important terms

- using outside sources but not giving them credit in the speech
- having too few specifics that you are under the time limit of the speech
- having too many specifics that you are over the time limit of the speech

Conclusion:

- neglecting to have a clear transition to the conclusion
- not re-emphasizing the central idea of the speech
- failing to review the main points of the speech to help the audience remember them
- having an overly long conclusion that puts the speech over the time limit
- saying something like, "That's it. I'm done." instead of having a strong closer
- not thanking the audience for their attention
- not asking the audience if they have any questions

How to deal with "flubs" or interruptions during the speech: We all experience little slips of the tongue during a speech—from "spoonerisms" (switching the first sounds of two words—for example calling a good person a "pood gerson"), to mispronouncing a name, to being unable to spit out the simplest words that you would normally have no trouble saying. The pressure public speaking puts on a person will occasionally cause these little flubs, so don't panic when they inevitably happen to you.

The worst way to deal with a flub is to panic

and make a big deal out of it. If you get upset or embarrassed or ask your audience if you can start your speech over again, then you will make the moment much bigger than it needs to be. You'll have a hard time getting the speech flowing again after such a moment, and your audience will remember your reaction to the flub even more than they will remember the main points of the speech.

The best strategy for dealing with flubs is to call as little attention to them as you can. This can be difficult, but you should try not to get worked up over the mistake. Usually all you need to do is take a few seconds to get your bearings, say "excuse me," correct your flub, then move on with the speech. You might even want to chuckle just a bit at your flub as a way of telling the audience that it's okay for them to share the humor of your flub. We're all human beings, right? If you handle the flub with calm grace, your audience will completely forget about it in about 30 seconds, and their focus will be back where you want it to be: on the content of your speech.

Dealing with an interruption is similar. If someone enters or leaves the room during your speech, generally it's best to ignore the person and not let him or her interfere with your speech. Even if the person is making noise or being rude, he or she will usually either be gone or seated in a few seconds, so it's best to let the moment pass naturally. If you are feeling especially confident, go ahead and say hello to the new arrival, welcoming the person to the group.

If someone interrupts your speech to ask a question or dispute a point, you have two options. If you can give a clear answer in a few words, then go ahead and briefly answer the question before going back to the substance of your speech. But if the question would take too long to answer adequately at that point, politely inform the questioner that you will give the question a full answer during the question-and-answer session at the end of your speech.

Speakers do sometimes run into a heckler during a speech. Although the fear of encountering a heckler is a big source of anxiety to inexperienced public speakers, this is actually a very rare occurrence. If you actually are heckled during a speech, it isn't really your responsibility to deal with the person. In fact, the audience itself and, especially, the organizers of the event where you are speaking (teacher, boss, etc.) are responsible for dealing with the heckler so that you can give the speech you have been asked to give.

Using Handouts and Visual Aids

Most public speaking occasions are fairly "low-tech." You might not always have access to computerized presentation software and equipment, document cameras, models, charts, or even a chalkboard. If you do have access to these resources, then, by all means, use them to your advantage. Computerized presentation software, in particular, has become a standard feature on basic computer systems. Bookstores or the Internet will have guidebooks for using these software programs, and most colleges or local adult-education programs offer classes on their use. (Here is one essential piece of advice for using presentation software that can't be ignored: *Never* simply project a paragraph of words onto the screen and read it aloud. That's a strategy guaranteed to make your audience sleepy, hostile, or both.)

In the more common, low-tech public speaking situations, you can always use a handout. Handouts can be as simple as one sheet of paper copied before the speech and distributed to every member of your audience. Your handout should have some kind of *visual appeal*, provide the *central theme* of the speech near the top, list the *main points* of the speech in the order they are presented, and include information that identifies the *source* of the information. A handout like this can have several important benefits:

- It helps your audience follow along during the speech.
- It helps your audience remember your main points after the speech.
- It gives your audience a concrete item to take with them and share with others.
- It establishes your authority by showing that you have worked to prepare for the speech.
- It helps eliminate boredom during the speech by giving listeners something to keep their focus if their minds wander.
- It gives the audience something to look at during the speech besides you!

If possible, have your handouts distributed to the audience before you give your speech. Passing them out as you begin your speech is okay, but that can be distracting and eat up a lot of time. Besides, there are many good ways to make an impression on your audience with a grabber at the beginning of your speech, rather than awkwardly taking up time passing out your handout. Generally, you'll be better off if you avoid giving your audience extensive handouts with multiple pages of dense information. Less is more—especially with a handout that focuses on the main points of your speech. In these days when people are often forced to do more work with fewer resources, your audience members probably won't have time to read extensive handouts—and they might wonder where you got the budget to do so much copying!

Figures 1 and 2 provide examples of handouts that could be used for a speech. Figure 1 might be for a fairly brief "show-and-tell" speech that explains the reasons why people are afraid of public speaking (see Section One). The use of unusual "frightening" fonts (from top to bottom—scratch-my-back, earthquake, beast wars, and brad) emphasizes the theme of "fear" in public speaking. Copying the handout on bright red paper might further reflect the theme of anxiety. You could even use some clip art (skull and crossbones, bats, etc.) for more low-tech fright value to make the handout attention-getting and entertaining for your audience. (Note: Simple fonts are usually best for handouts because they are easiest to read. If you use an unusual font, make sure that it's readable and has a connection with your speech topic.)

Figure 2 is a handout for a longer persuasive presentation at an academic conference focused on convincing teacher to adopt strategies for avoiding professional burnout. Copying the handout on the presenter's college letterhead gives it a clean, professional appearance and provides good public relations for the college. Both handouts provide the central theme of the speech at the top of the page and list the main points of each speech in a rough outline format, and both include an element of visual appeal as well as information identifying their sources.

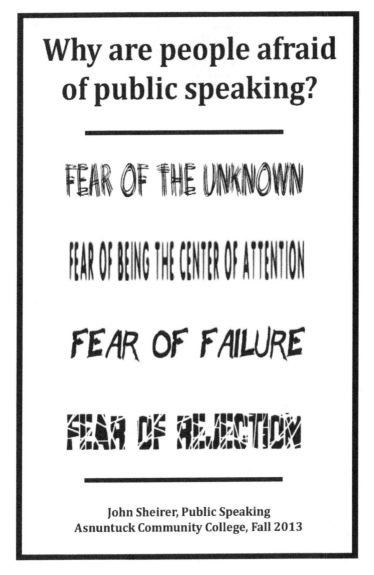

Figure 1: Audience handout that emphasizes the main points of a speech.

ASNUNTUCK
COMMUNITY COLLEGE

Ten Strategies for Reinvigorating Community College English Faculty

John Sheirer, Asnuntuck Community College

Source of burnout: We can't always tell if we're making a difference for our students.
Strategy #1: Focus on your impact on students beyond the classroom.

Source of burnout: Sometimes our students seem like they don't want to learn basic grammar.
Strategy #2: Give up the battle to save the English language from the march of time.

Source of burnout: It's easy to feel a sense of powerlessness in the overall curriculum.
Strategy #3: Get involved with writing across the curriculum initiatives.

Source of burnout: We sometimes forget the power of writing.
Strategy #4: Make writing a more integrated part of our everyday lives.

Source of burnout: Writing is hard work, both for us and for our students.
Strategy #5: Start a personal blog and a class blog.

Source of burnout: Too much "business" keeps us from connecting with our colleagues.
Strategy #6: Have department meetings without a business agenda.

Source of burnout: We don't get enough feedback from our colleagues and supervisors.
Strategy #7: Praise our colleagues' good works.

Source of burnout: We are often disconnected from our academic specialty.
Strategy #8: Do something in our specialty outside of the classroom.

Source of burnout: We have such heavy loads in teaching composition.
Strategy #9: Take a graduate course specifically in the teaching of composition.

Source of burnout: Our own expectations can be unreasonably high.
Strategy #10: Learn the community college English teacher serenity prayer.

Figure 2: Audience handout that emphasizes the main points of a speech.

Using main points and details to make your speaking notes: Public speakers are at their best when speaking *extemporaneously*. This means speaking to an audience in much the same manner as we speak in conversation—not word-for-word from a manuscript or memorized the way an actor recites lines in a play. Extemporaneous speaking requires lots of practice with special attention to the main points and details of the speech.

The best kind of speaking notes to use during an extemporaneous speech is one 8.5"x11" sheet of paper with the main points of the speech written out in simple, easy-to-read, large-print key words, followed by a few sub-point key words written in smaller print. (Often your audience handout, with some essential details added to the list of main points, works well for speaking notes.) Use these notes not just for delivering the speech itself, but also for practicing the speech. You should practice your speech enough in advance that you only have to glance at your notes occasionally, focusing most of your concentration on your audience.

The primary advantage to a list of main points is that you don't need to look at it much so that you can maintain eye-contact with your audience. Other performance aspects of public speaking also are easier when speaking to the audience, and you can concentrate on putting energy and personality into the speech when your attention is not fixed on your notes. And the content of the speech is often more organized when you focus on identifying main points for your speaking notes.

Some speakers prefer using index cards for speaking notes, listing one main point and a few details on each card. The advantage of index cards is that they won't flop around the way a full sheet of paper might, and they are smaller and less obtrusive. On the other hand, index cards also have some disadvantages. Because index cards are small, the notes written on them must be small, sometimes requiring a speaker to lift the card close to the face, squint, or stare to read it. This interferes with maintaining strong eye-contact with your audience (and can make you look a bit silly). Cards can also get out of sequence if they are not painstakingly arranged before the speech, sometimes causing a panicked speaker to lose his or her place. And cards require a great deal of shuffling during a speech, possibly preventing expressive, natural gesturing.

The disadvantages of reading or memorizing your speech: Inexperienced public speakers often mistakenly believe that they should read word-for-word from a manuscript version of the speech, written out in advance. (The manuscript speech, discussed in Section Four, is meant to be read word-for-word, but it is an exception that usually involves reading a manuscript written by someone other than the speaker.)

There is only one major advantage to reading your entire speech from a manuscript: you will never find yourself wondering what to say next. Unfortunately, that is where the advantages to this strategy end. Several very serious problems can occur when reading the speech from a manuscript:

- First, making adequate eye-contact with your audience when looking at a manuscript is very difficult.
- Second, the speaker's voice will often be aimed down at the paper rather than projected out to the audience.

- Third, even if the speaker doesn't lose his or her place, there will often be awkward points when a sentence is read in a halting manner.
- And, finally, it is very difficult to invest any "personality" into a speech that is simply read from the pages of a manuscript, often making the speech seem dull or boring.

Only extremely talented, experienced public speakers can read a speech from a manuscript and deliver an effective speech. Some politicians, former President Bill Clinton, for example, can give a very effective speech when reading from a manuscript. But he is a very skilled speaker who has given hundreds of speeches each year for decades. In contrast, most speakers who use word-for-word manuscripts have a very difficult time. The next time you see a speaker read from a manuscript during a speech, ask yourself how effective the performance is, especially compared to a speaker who talks directly to an audience with a list of main points used as notes.

Beginning public speakers are also tempted to memorize their speeches word-for-word. Unless you have a perfect memory, this is extremely difficult and can lead to embarrassment if even one part of the speech is forgotten. And, as is the case with reading from a manuscript, investing a memorized speech with emotion and energy is more the job of an actor than a public speaker.

Sample speaking notes: Figure 3 shows a sample of effective public speaking notes for a speech about the reasons why people are afraid of public speaking. It is adapted directly from a handout of main points that could be distributed to the audience during the speech (see Figure 1 earlier in this section), with some of the most important details filled in to help prompt the speaker's memory. These details could actually be handwritten on the handout itself and refined by the speaker during practice sessions delivering the speech. You could also add performance guidelines in the margins as reminders to yourself to smile or project your voice. When you use this approach to speaking notes, be sure to follow two key guidelines: make the details are *legible* and make them *big enough* that you don't have to look too long at the notes that you lose eye-contact time with your audience.

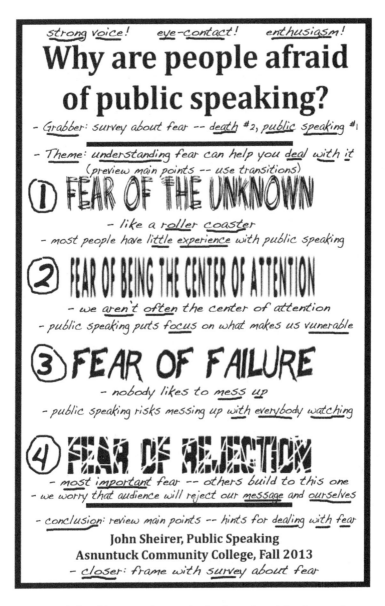

Figure 3: Speaking notes that emphasize the main points of a speech.

Thinking During the Speech

Inexperienced public speakers often believe that good public speakers think only about their speeches while giving their speeches, but this is far from true. It is very easy for your mind to wander off on one tangent while your mouth follows the organizational pattern of the speech that you have practiced extensively. Your mouth might be calmly talking about the need to put money in steady-growth investments to see a long-term return, but your brain might be screaming to you about how much you hate being in front of an audience, or questioning why everyone in the audience looks so bored, or panicking because you think you might have a piece of food stuck between your front teeth. Or you might just be thinking that your feet ache and wondering if your friends are enjoying the road trip to a concert that you missed because you had to give a speech.

This kind of mental panic or distraction is very common, so don't feel bad if you suffer from it. But instead of letting an active mental process undermine your speech, use it to enhance your performance. If you feel your mind wander or begin to suspect that your audience is bored, punch up the speech with some expressive hand gestures or change the volume of your voice to recapture the audience's attention and your own focus. Dismiss the useless stream-of-consciousness stuff and concentrate on what helps you as a speaker. In other words, use the four aspects of public speaking performance: voice, eye-contact, body language, and "personality" put into the speech.

Processing the Experience
After the Speech

Once the speech is completed, you should try to organize your thoughts about how the experience went. This can best be done by jotting down a few reflective freewriting notes about the speech, particularly centered around the performance and content of the speech. How was your voice? Your eye-contact? Your body language? Your "personality" put into the speech? How was your introduction? Your organization? Your development? Your conclusion? Make an honest assessment of the experience and ask yourself what you can do to improve when you give your next speech. If you are given feedback from a teacher, supervisor, or classmate after the speech, examine how that feedback matches or doesn't match what the speech felt like to you. If the speech was videotaped, watch the video and see how the speech looked from the audience's perspective (without judging yourself too harshly on your appearance, as we all tend to do—remember, everyone looks heavier on video and has a bad hair day now and then!). Doing reflective writing can help you learn as much as possible from the experience of giving the speech.

The form shown in Figure 4 can help you evaluate your own speech. From top to bottom, the form covers the most important aspects of public speaking performance. From left to right, it covers public speaking strengths and weaknesses. This one-page form summarized pretty much everything from the previous sections of the book about the important concepts of public speaking performance and content.

You can use checks in the blanks to indicate

that a particular strength or weakness happens sometimes or with moderate intensity. And pluses can indicate that the area happens often or with a great deal of intensity. For example, if your grabber fully captures the audience at the beginning of the speech, then put a plus sign next to "strong grabber" in the left column. If you scanned the room and made eye-contact with most of the audience, but you could improve your coverage of certain areas of the room, then put a check mark next to "saw whole audience" on the left. If you hinted at introducing your main points near the end of your introduction but didn't preview them clearly, then put a check mark beside "main points not clearly previewed" on the right. And if you realize that your speech rambled and had no main points or transitions at all, then put a plus sign in all of the blanks on the right side under "organization."

Fill out the form yourself based on your memory of giving the speech, or, better yet, while watching a video of your speech. Be honest but gentle with yourself. You might also have a friend, coworker, classmate, or instructor fill out this form to give you feedback on your speech. (You can also use this form to get feedback when practicing your speech before presenting it formally.) Explain the concepts of performance and content to the person providing feedback, and encourage this person to be as honest as possible so that you get a clear indication of your abilities. As you progress as a public speaker, focus on keeping your strengths strong and improving your adequate and weak areas.

Name _____ Speech Type _____ Time _____ Too Long _ Too Short _ Just Right _

√ = some   + = very much

Strengths   ## Weaknesses

• Performance •

Voice

__ strong volume   __ too quiet/too loud
__ projected well to audience   __ projected down/up too much
__ well paced   __ too fast/too slow
__ good pronunciation   __ too many verbalized pauses

Eye-contact

__ saw whole audience   __ looked down too much
__ held eye-contact throughout speech   __ looked at one or few places too much
__ connected with audience through eye-contact __ looked over audience heads

Body language

__ relaxed/natural body language   __ distracting mannerisms
__ good stance   __ slouching/rigid posture
__ used gestures for emphasis   __ no/too few/too many gestures

"Personality" put into the speech

__ energetic and enthusiastic   __ need more energy/enthusiasm/authority
__ looked confident   __ looked nervous
__ projected authority   __ read from manuscript too much
__ connected with audience through smile   __ should smile more

• Content •

Introduction

__ strong grabber/well-delivered grabber   __ no/weak grabber/poorly delivered grabber
__ introduced topic and central idea well   __ topic and central idea not clearly introduced
__ previewed main points   __ main points not clearly previewed

Organization

__ main points clearly stated   __ main points unclear
__ main points well emphasized   __ main points not emphasized
__ main points well ordered   __ main points disorganized
__ transitions clear   __ no/unclear transitions

Development

__ clear specific details   __ too many/too few specific details
__ specific details connected to main points   __ specific details not connected with main points
__ unfamiliar terms well defined   __ unfamiliar terms not defined
__ sources acknowledged   __ sources not acknowledged

Conclusion

__ clear transition to conclusion   __ no/unclear transition to conclusion
__ re-emphasized topic and central idea   __ topic and central idea not clearly re-emphasized
__ reviewed main points   __ main points not clearly reviewed
__ strong closer/well-delivered closer   __ no/weak closer/poorly delivered closer
__ thanked audience   __ did not thank audience
__ asked for questions   __ did not ask for questions

Figure 4: Feedback and evaluation form for the performance and content of a speech.

Section Four:
The Major Types of Speeches

Not all public speaking situations are the same. Each calls for different strategies for effective speeches. You can prepare for just about every public speaking situation in which you might find yourself if you first analyze the speaking situation and decide what type of speech is most appropriate. Almost all public speaking situations can be broken down into six basic types:

The six major types of speeches:

- *Introduction speech:* introducing a living or historical person
- *"Show-and-tell" speech:* using a simple prop to help explain a more complex subject
- *Demonstration speech:* explaining and showing how to do a process
- *Persuasion speech:* attempting to educate and influence your audience about an issue
- *Impromptu speech:* giving a speech with little or no preparation time
- *Manuscript speech:* presenting word-for-word a speech where the text is already written

Rarely (if ever) does a public speaker actually say, "You know, I think I'd like to do a 'show-and-tell' speech at today's staff meeting." Instead, someone might be asked (or required) to speak to a group of people but not be given many specific guidelines about how to approach the speech. Selecting the type of speech you should do and using the guidelines included in this section can be like selecting the proper tool to do a job. Being aware of different speech types can help you select which tool you need, and then studying the guidelines for the speech type (along with the general guidelines provided in Sections Two and Three of this book) can show you how to best use the tool.

It's important to note that there is often overlap between types of speeches. These are not exclusive categories with no blending. A "show-and-tell" speech might very well have elements of persuasion or demonstration, for example. A speaker shouldn't try to squeeze a speech into a certain type just for the sake of making it fit. Don't be afraid to mix types a bit if it is appropriate for the speaking situation, especially as you develop your skills as a speaker.

This section focuses on each of these six speech types, defines the speech type, names the specific public speaking skill most needed for each type of speech, lists some examples of each type of speech, details the qualities of an effective speech of each type, explains the most common problems of each speech type, gives organizational guidance for each type of speech, and provides a practice assignment for each type of speech.

Introduction Speech

What is an Introduction Speech?

An introduction speech presents a living (or sometimes historical) individual to a group in a way that provides relevant facts, builds audience acceptance, respect, and enthusiasm, and helps create a sense of welcome.

Key Public Speaking Skills Needed for an Introduction Speech

- Creating connections between individuals and groups.

Examples of Introduction Speeches

- a community organizer introduces a city official at a rally
- an officer of an organization briefly introduces the main speaker at a special event
- a supervisor introduces a visiting guest at a work site
- a presenter introduces someone receiving an award or special recognition
- a historian tells about an important historical person by introducing the person as if she were still alive

The Qualities of an Effective Introduction Speech

* *An effective introduction speech is organized around clear main points and details about the subject:*

The body of an introduction speech includes, of course, information about your subject, the person being introduced. How that information is presented in the body of the speech is a key to making the speech effective. Most of an the speech should present clear main points about the subject in a logical order, with specific details to illuminate those main points. The main points are the "big ideas" about the person being introduced that provide the framework or outline of the speech, while the details are the specifics that fill out the speech.

For example, if you are introducing a school athlete who is being honored with an award at a banquet, you might have three main points: that the athlete is a great player, a strong leader, and a well-rounded person. These three main points would provide the outline of the speech. To fill in the details, you would provide specific examples from the athlete's career to illustrate these three main points. To show that the person is a great player, for instance, you might list overall accomplishments, statistics, or accounts of outstanding specific games or plays. Details attesting to the athlete's leadership abilities might include accounts from teammates that show how the athlete lead them to accomplish great things as a team. And the main point that the athlete is a well-rounded person could be detailed with information about off-the-field activities and accomplishments, such as academic achievements, volunteer work, or outstanding abilities in other areas like music or the debate team.

- *An effective introduction speech is factually accurate:*

Very few things about life in general (or public speaking specifically) need to be perfect, but your main points and details about the subject should be as close to perfectly accurate as possible. Errors of fact can be embarrassing for both the speaker and the subject. For example, introducing someone who has twenty years of experience in his or her field by saying the person has five years of experience will usually make that person correct the speaker, getting his or her speech off to a bad start.

Facts must be checked and double-checked, often directly with the person being introduced, before the speech is given. You should also pay particular attention to the spelling and pronunciation of the subject's name, a very important fact. No one likes to hear his or her name get mangled in an introduction. (Author's special note: My last name, Sheirer, is pronounced "shy-err." I can't even begin to count how many times and how many ways my name has been mispronounced by well-meaning but unprepared speakers who have introduced me.)

- *An effective introduction speech is appropriate for the occasion and the audience:*

All speeches should be appropriate for the occasion and audience, but this quality takes on a special meaning for an introduction speech. You should consider the reason that the person is being introduced and make the information provided appropriate to that reason.

For example, if the person being introduced is a consultant who will work with a group of employees to help solve a specific problem, then the introduction should include information about the person's background dealing with similar problems. If the person is an environmental expert who will give a presentation about recycling, then the speech should focus on the person's expertise in recycling.

The tone of the introduction should also be appropriate. If the occasion is a festive one, the tone should be upbeat. If the occasion is serious, the tone should mirror that seriousness. If that occasion is sad, the tone should be appropriately poignant.

You should also assess the demographics (age, background, attitudes, etc.) of the audience and tailor the speech to that audience. For example, if the audience is composed primarily of children, you should avoid overly "grown-up" material in the introduction. An assessment of demographics is very important for any speech, but it can be especially important for an introduction speech that needs to connect the audience with the person being introduced. For instance, if the audience has only limited technical knowledge of the subject's area of expertise, you should avoid talking "over the head" of the audience.

- *An effective introduction speech is respectful of the subject:*

You shouldn't put down the person being introduced (except in the special case of a "roast" where speakers poke fun at the subject in a good-natured, tongue-in-cheek manner). You also shouldn't reveal inappropriate personal information given by the subject in confidence, no matter how well you might know the person.

For example, if you are introducing a classmate who you know just went through a messy divorce, that information should definitely not be part of your introduction without clearing that revelation with the subject first. You might be letting the class know an important fact about your subject, but it certainly wouldn't make the person feel comfortable with the group. Eventually, the person might wish to reveal that information, but your job as an introducer is not to make that choice for your subject.

- *An effective introduction speech is suspenseful, creative, surprising, or in some way entertaining:*

Introduction speeches must be more than simple lists of facts. The best of these speeches weave the facts into an interesting framework that keeps the audience attentive. Introduction speeches should reveal something about the personality of the person being introduced, as well as something about the person making the introduction speech. You don't need to be a stand-up comedian or expert storyteller, but you should try to make the introduction a positive experience for the subject and the audience.

For example, suppose you have to introduce a visiting geneticist whom you never even met before picking him up at the airport the day of the speech. You would certainly have done your research on this person, so you would have lots of facts to present to your audience in the introduction. But even the most interesting facts about the person's work in genetics might strike the audience as just a bit dull. So you might add an element of entertainment to the introduction by dovetailing these facts with a story about the geneticist showing you pictures of his children (the product of a different kind of genetic activity) on the drive back from the airport.

Most Common Problems with an Introduction Speech

Taking too much time and telling too much about the subject: When you introduce someone who will be giving a speech, the emphasis should be on the main speaker, not on the person making the introduction. Your introduction should take only a fraction of the time the main speaker has for his or her speech. So if you are introducing a speaker who will be giving a half-hour presentation, for instance, you shouldn't take up more than a few minutes for the introduction.

Creating unrealistic expectations of the subject by overpraising: Although you often want to praise the person you are introducing, too much praise is difficult for even the most outstanding person to live up to. For example, if you introduce a visiting consultant as "the woman who has single-handedly save hundreds of companies from financial ruin," or call her "the Jesus Christ of consultants," then anything less than a miracle from that consultant will be disappointing (and many members of your audience might find your comparison a bit offensive).

Introduction Speech Structure

In general, the outline for an introduction speech should follow the basic structure shown below. (See the guidelines for organizing a speech in Section Three for basic information about how to structure a speech.)

- *Introduction:*
  - Grabber
  - Preview the central theme of the speech
  - Preview the main points of the speech

- *Body (use this order for each main point):*
  - Transition to the main point about the subject
  - State and emphasize the main point
  - Provide details about the main point

- *Conclusion:*
  - Transition to the conclusion
  - Re-emphasize the central theme of the speech
  - Review the main points of speech
  - Closer

- *Introduction:*

Grabber: Get your audience's attention by beginning the speech strongly, perhaps with a question related to the person you are introducing, a dramatic statement about the person, or a quote from your conversations with the person.

Preview the central theme of the speech: Let your audience know the central theme or focus of your introduction speech—for example, that everyone in your class will enjoy working with the person or that the person is very knowledgeable in the field.

Preview the main points of speech: Give a general roadmap of your introduction speech. This could be done by listing the main points you plan to make about the person, possibly by mentioning that the person receiving an award for the arts has done great work in three areas: as a singer, writer, and actor. Or you could hit the highlights of what you will cover in the body of the speech if there are many main points in a longer speech (a brief summary of the person's accomplishments in his or her field of expertise, for example).

- *Body* (use this order for each main point):

Transition to the main point about the subject: Guide your audience through the main points of the speech. For example, when covering the person's work life in your main points, you could use transitions such as "first, during her early career," "later, as she became well-established," and "recently, in her current position."

State and emphasize the main point: After saying the transition, speak the main point, emphasize it strongly, pause for clarity, and repeat the point if necessary. For a main point showing that the person cares about family, state very strongly, "Bill is an exceptional family man … (brief pause for emphasis) … His family is very important to him … (brief pause for emphasis) … Without his family, he would not be the person he is today."

Provide details about the main point: Bring the

general main point to life with specific details. The main point about the importance of family for the person being introduced, for instance, could be illustrated with facts (the names of his spouse and children, and the children's ages) and anecdotes (a few brief stories illustrating the importance of his family).

- *Conclusion*

Transition to conclusion: Signal that the speech is almost over with the standard, "in conclusion," or something more creative and specific to the introduction speech, such as, "So, what have we learned about Danielle Barone, our new Sales Director?"

Re-emphasize the central theme of the speech: Go back to the main focus of the speech to make sure that it has connected with the audience. For example, say, "As you get to know Roger, you'll see why he is going to be a strong addition to our orchestra's string section."

Review the main points of the speech: Either list the main points again to be certain that the audience has them all ("Let me just repeat the three qualities that Yusef brings to our management team…creativity, a strong computer background, and great people skills") or simply summarize the main points ("Sally's education and experience will make her a fine addition to our faculty.").

Closer: Close the speech with a bang, perhaps connecting back to the grabber to frame the speech with a particularly striking specific detail about your subject.

Introduction Speech
Practice Assignment

Introduce one of your classmates to the rest of the class. Your job is to get the class to be pleased that this person is in the class, help the person feel welcome, and present at least the following information in an entertaining way: where your subject is from, what other courses he or she is taking, educational or career goals the person has, any public speaking experience the person has had, and at least three main points that make the person interesting, distinctive, or unique.

"Show-and-Tell" Speech

What is a "Show-and-Tell" Speech?

A "show-and-tell" speech is an explanation speech that uses some kind of object or prop to help explain a larger idea, observation, or experience related to that object. The speaker focuses primarily on explaining the larger subject, not just the object itself.

Key Public Speaking Skill Needed for a "Show-and-Tell" Speech

Using a prop as a springboard to explain a more complex idea, observation, or experience.

Examples of Show-and-Tell" Speeches

- a student uses a model to explain a natural phenomenon such as a volcano
- an employee explains the purpose of a new piece of equipment
- a parent shows photos of himself as a teenager to his own children as a way to begin explaining the social issues of the recent past
- a war veteran explains the significance of a battlefield souvenir
- an athlete uses her "lucky socks" to help explain athletic superstitions

The Qualities of an Effective "Show-and-Tell" Speech

- *An effective "show-and-tell" speech is organized around clear main points and details about the larger subject:*

The body of the "show-and-tell" speech should present clear, well-ordered main points about the subject, with specific details to develop those main points. The main points are the "big ideas" that provide the framework or outline of the speech, while the details are the specifics that make the main points more understandable and fill out the speech.

For example, you might do a "show-and-tell" speech in an ecology class where your prop is a collection of shells from the beach and the larger subject you are explaining is your experience visiting your grandparents' home on the Maine coast last summer. Your main points might be the five most important things you learned about New England costal environments. If your first main point is that New England beaches are filled with a great variety of sea life, the details you present for that main point would be a specific list and descriptions of the different forms of sea life living on and around that beach. Your other four main points in the speech would be similarly developed with appropriate details.

- *An effective "show-and-tell" speech has a well-presented, interesting object that clearly connects to the larger subject before being explained:*

You can present and describe an object (or objects) so that the entire audience can see it (as well as hear, touch, smell, or taste it, if appropriate) and understand exactly what it is. If the object is fairly large, (a poster, perhaps) you should hold it up for the audience to see. If it is small (for instance, a photograph) you should pass it around the audience so everyone can experience it. A volunteer helper is often helpful for passing things around the audience while you focus on the speech itself.

You have to also make a clear connection between the object and the larger subject being explained. For example, if you use a religious medal to explain a specific belief, then you must be sure that the audience understands the relationship between the medal and the belief. And in the earlier example of the speech about the New England seacoast, you should be able to connect some of the beach life that you describe with some of the shells that you use as a prop to get your audience thinking about the beach.

Note: You can do an explanation-type speech without a prop, but the prop, when used effectively, can get the audience connected and involved more fully than when you forego the prop.

- *An effective "show-and-tell" speech is focused on the larger subject being explained (not the object being presented):*

While the prop is important, a "show-and-tell" speech won't be fully effective if it is only about the object being presented. Remember that your ultimate goal in a "show-and-tell" speech is to explain a larger subject. The object is primarily a prop to get and hold the audience's attention and get them thinking about the larger subject. Too much emphasis on the object makes the speech more like a technical report than an explanation of a larger subject.

For example, if you have ten minutes to present a marketing campaign for a new toy to the advertising copywriters and designers, but you spend most of the speech talking about the toy itself, the larger subject of the marketing campaign will not be as developed as it needs to be for your audience. Focusing most of the speech on the larger subject—the marketing campaign itself—will better aid the copywriters and designers in understanding that marketing campaign.

- *An effective "show-and-tell" speech is revealing about the speaker's personal connection to the object and larger subject being explained:*

"Show-and-tell" speeches not only look at the object and a larger subject; they tell the audience something important about the speaker as well. This can make the difference between dull and lively content in a "show-and-tell" speech.

For example, an armed-services veteran using a gas mask as a springboard to help explain the larger subject of "Gulf War Syndrome" would make a speech more interesting by explaining that she wore that particular mask every day for an entire tour of duty on the front lines of the Gulf War. Failing to mention this fact as part of the speech would take away a great deal of the speaker's personal authority and vitality, making the speech seem more distant and dry than it should.

- *An effective "show-and-tell" speech is appropriate for the audience and connected with the audience's experience:*

Demographics play an important role in selecting an appropriate prop and larger subject for a "show-and-tell" speech. Obviously, an object with sexual implications would be inappropriate for children's groups (as well as many adult groups). In addition, an analysis of the attitudes and beliefs of an audience can aid in selecting an appropriate prop. For example, photographs of aborted fetuses will never help a pro-choice audience member understand the pro-life viewpoint, only make that audience member distrust and dislike the speaker.

Most people have attended speeches where the speaker seems to have little or no idea who the audience is. Clearly that can lead to poor speech-making. To whatever extent possible, a speaker should research the audience before the speech and try to use an object that audience members are likely to recognize and enjoy. For example, if a company invites a motivational speaker to address employees on the topic of leadership in organizations, and that speaker uses one of the company's products as a prop to generate audience interest, then the audience is likely to appreciate the speaker's message more than if the speaker used props only from his or her own experience.

Most Common Problems with a "Show-and-Tell" Speech

Focusing too much on the object and not enough on the larger subject: Excessive attention on the object takes the emphasis away from where it really belongs, on explaining whatever idea, observation, or experience constitutes the larger subject. The object itself is a prop to generate interest in or promote understanding of the topic—not the topic itself. [Note: Sometimes you may wish to explain an object—a computer, for example. In that case, the computer is the larger subject, so you may wish to have a different prop to capture your audience's attention. Also, if your goal is to explain how an object works, you might wish to consider a demonstration speech (see details later in this section) rather than "show-and-tell".]

Failing to indicate the connection between the object and the larger subject: If an audience has no idea why you keep waving a tie-dyed shirt or a set of keys or a stuffed animal over your head, whatever you're trying to say about a larger subject will be lost as confused audience members try to figure out the connection for themselves. Sometimes in the anxiety of giving a speech, you may realize that you've forgotten to show your object at the start of the speech as you had intended. If you find yourself in this situation, don't beg the audience to let you start over. Instead, simply present the object as soon as you can in a way that connects it with the central theme of the speech.

"Show-and-Tell" Speech Structure

In general, the outline for a "show-and-tell" speech should follow the basic structure shown below. (See the guidelines for organizing a speech in Section Three for basic information about how to structure any speech.)

- *Introduction:*
  - Grabber
  - Present the connection between the object and the larger subject
  - Present the central theme of the speech
  - Preview the main points of the speech

- *Body (use this order for each main point):*
  - Transition to the main point
  - State and emphasize the main point
  - Provide details about the main point

- *Conclusion:*
  - Transition to the conclusion
  - Re-emphasize the central theme of the speech
  - Review the main points of the speech
  - Closer

- *Introduction:*

Grabber: The object you use to get your audience focused on your larger subject makes a simple and natural grabber for a "show-and-tell" speech. Puns, usually considered a low form of humor unless used subtly, can be effective grabbers in a "show-and-tell" speech because they can create a connection between your object and larger subject. For example, you might hold up a set of keys for your audience to see at the beginning of your speech on personal finances and explain that your speech will show the audience the five "keys" to financial freedom. Or you could make the grabber humorous, holding up a bra or jock strap as a grabber for a speech about a time your friends gave you the "support" you needed in a difficult situation. (Please note, however, that the use of somewhat "off-color" grabbers such as this one can be effective only if you have researched your audience enough to know that they won't be offended by such a grabber.)

Present the connection between the object and the larger subject: Make sure that the connection between the object you use for your grabber and the larger subject your speech will focus on is clear. Some connections (such as the key mentioned above) don't need much explanation. But other connections might be a bit less direct and more metaphorical, so you must provide enough direction to keep your audience from being confused by your object.

Present the central theme of the speech: "Show-and-tell" speeches don't focus on the object; that's just a prop to get people's attention. The real focus is some larger subject—an idea or observation that is important to you or an experience that had an impact on you. What you think of that idea or observation or experience is the central theme to the "show-and-tell" speech. Your introduction should present this central theme. You might say about an idea, for instance, "Freedom of speech is not just a right, but a responsibility." The bulk of your speech will in some way relate back to that central idea. If your speech focuses on an observation, you might present the central theme like this: "Watching reality TV shows has taught me that American culture is in decline." Or in a speech about an experience, you might present the central theme by noting that "My whole life changed on the day that my first daughter was born."

Preview the main points of the speech: A brief "show-and-tell" speech might have only three or four main points about your subject included in the body. In that case, list them at the end of your introduction. A longer speech might have a great many points, so you can summarize them rather than listing them. In either case, previewing the main points just before you launch into the body of the speech will help your audience follow the speech as it develops.

- *Body* (use this order for each main point):

   Transition to the main point: Use "signpost" words—such as "first," "second," "third" or "most important," "most noticeable," "most frightening," etc.—to guide your readers through the main points you make about your subject in the body of your speech.
   State and emphasize the main point: Your speech's main points—the big ideas that you have to say about your topic—create the outline of the speech's body. For instance, the main points of a "show-and-tell" speech about why a particular summer job was so fulfilling to you might include how much you learned at that job, how much fun you had at that job, and how many new friends you made at that job. You would emphasize all of these main points by stating them strongly as you come to them, restating them for further emphasis, and pausing a bit after stating them. In a sense, you should emphasize the way you state your main points in very much the same way underlining or bold print emphasizes headings in a piece of writing (such as headings in this book). Without such emphasis, your audience might not catch the importance of your main points.

Provide details about the main point: Simply presenting a list of main points would form just an outline rather than an in-depth speech. That might be okay if your speech is only supposed to be thirty seconds or so. But most speeches need the depth provided by details connected to main points. For instance, if you are speaking about your observation of reality TV, and one main point is that the "characters" in the program seem more fake than real, you might present some research information showing that behind-the-scenes accounts of these shows reveal that the producers coach the characters into over-dramatizing situations. You might also conduct a survey among your friends showing that seven out of ten of them think that these kinds of shows usually seem unrealistic. These specific details do more than just fill time in a speech; they flesh out the main points so that your audience can fully understand what your main points mean.

• *Conclusion*

Transition to the conclusion: Signal the approaching end of your speech with a transitional phrase. "In conclusion" works as well as anything else. In a "show-and-tell" speech specifically, showing or mentioning the object again can help make the transition to your conclusion more effective.

Re-emphasize the central theme of the speech: Summarize the overall message of the speech again so that your audience has a better chance of remembering. For a speech about time management, for instance, the central theme might be, "Time management, like

111

making a speech fit our time limit, is something we all can do with just a little planning." Or a speech explaining an important experience on the first day of school might be summed up by saying, "That first day was a real transition to my life as an independent adult."

Review the main points of the speech: To assure that your audience comprehended the main points, review them at the end of the speech. If your speech covered three main points about the concept of what makes a great salesperson, then mention them again in your conclusion: "Remember, the three most important qualities of a great salesperson are tactful assertiveness, a customer focus, and knowledge of the product." Or the ten main points of a speech explaining the importance of the final football game of your high school career might be reviewed in summary rather than a long list by stating, "That game changed me as an athlete, a person, and a future coach."

Closer: Like any speech, the "show-and-tell" speech should end strongly. The "show-and-tell" speech, specifically, can come back to the object presented at the beginning of the speech to frame the content effectively. If your grabber included showing a set of keys to introduce an explanation of the five "keys" to financial freedom, bring out those keys at the end of the speech and identify them as car and house keys to show the buying power that financial freedom can provide. Connecting the grabber and closer through the "show-and-tell" object can emphasize the message of your speech while tying it together cleanly.

"Show-and-Tell" Speech
Practice assignment

Bring in an object that relates to a larger subject (idea, observation, or experience) that is important to you that you would like to explain to the class. The object can be anything—for example, photo, book, work of art, stuffed animal, sports equipment, tool, high-tech gizmo (no living creatures, please). Your job is to present the object to the class, define how the object connects to a larger subject, and explain the larger subject to the audience.

Demonstration Speech

What is a Demonstration Speech?

A demonstration speech shows an audience how to do a process in such a way that the audience can see how the process is done, understand how the process works, and remember enough about the process to try it for themselves.

Key Public Speaking Skills Needed for a Demonstration Speech

Analyzing a complex process and teaching that process to an audience.

Examples of Demonstration Speeches

- a supervisor shows an employee how to use a new piece of equipment
- a softball coach shows an infielder how to improve her throwing motion
- a student shows a class how to perform a chemistry lab experiment
- a rehabilitation therapist shows an accident victim how to walk with crutches
- parents show their children how to cook a meal *and* how to clean up afterward

The Qualities of an Effective Demonstration Speech

- *An effective demonstration speech is clearly organized around the main steps of the process being demonstrated:*

The main points in the body of a demonstration speech are the primary steps of the process being demonstrated. Your biggest job for this type of speech is analyzing the process to identify the most important steps, and then outlining the body of the speech around those steps.

For example, if you're demonstrating how to shoot a free throw in a basketball game, then you might identify these steps in the process as main points: 1) stepping to the free throw line, 2) receiving the ball from the referee, 3) sighting the rim, 4) flexing the knees, 5) taking a few dribbles, 6) positioning the ball in the hands, 7) positioning the arms for the shot, 8) releasing the shot, and 9) following through by snapping the wrist. You would emphasize the steps to break down the process and make it more memorable for the audience. These steps could also be outlined on a handout for the audience.

- *An effective demonstration speech includes clearly presented demonstrations of the main steps of the process:*

Demonstration is a visual skill. Talking about a process during a demonstration speech is important, but actually showing the process is even more important. If you only *tell* the audience how to do a process, the speech will not be anywhere near as effective as *showing* the process to the audience. The demonstrations of each step in the process must be done in such a way that the steps are visible to the audience and done slowly and clearly enough, or repeated often enough, that the audience can fully comprehend them.

You should maintain eye-contact as much as possible with the audience during demonstrations to stay connected with the audience. Maintaining eye-contact can be difficult while demonstrating a process, but eye-contact is still an essential element of performing the demonstration speech. You will need to practice your demonstrations a great deal and focus on being able to look at your audience a great deal while demonstrating. Of course, you are allowed to look down at your demonstrations during key moments, especially if those moments involve delicate equipment or sharp objects. Two useful strategies can help with maintaining eye-contact during demonstrations. One is learning your demonstrations so well that you don't need to look down too much while you do them, and the other is looking away from your audience and at your demonstrations only when it is essential for you to see what you are doing.

Also, you should continue talking during demonstrations. When audience members can both *see* and *hear* how to do a process, they are more likely to remember how to do it. (In addition, the best way to make this type of speech boring is to have long periods of silence during demonstrations.)

Showing how to deal with mistakes that might be made while attempting the process is also useful for the audience. For example, if you are demonstrating how to use a new photocopier, then you should actually show how to insert the paper, how to press the buttons, how to open the machine and remove a paper jam—and what to do in case the wrong button is pushed or the wrong paper inserted. Simply telling the audience how to do these steps while ignoring potential mistakes isn't enough.

- *An effective demonstration speech has lots of specific, practical information about the process and materials:*

Being able to provide information about the process being demonstrated serves two purposes. First, it allows you to transfer needed information about the process to help the audience understand and remember how to do the process. And second, it helps you fill in the brief periods of silence that often occur during demonstrations. (Notice, for example, how much useful information those talkative chefs on television cooking shows provide about the foods they're cooking!) In an organizational sense, the steps of the process provide the main points of the speech while the "tidbits" of information provide details to develop those main points.

For example, during a speech about the proper methods for brushing and flossing teeth, you could include information about what happens when people don't brush and floss, what the best types of floss and toothbrushes are, how the speaker came to be an expert on brushing and flossing, and any number of other tidbits that can fill silent time and help the audience understand the process.

- *An effective demonstration speech provides a description of the supplies, tools, and time needed for the process:*

The introduction of a demonstration speech is very much like the top of an online food recipe, providing a list of supplies, tools, and time needed for the process. This information is essential to an audience if they are to attempt the process on their own, and it is helpful to have this information included on a handout for the audience.

For example, a demonstration speech about making a "three-egg overstuffed omelet" would include a list of food ingredients needed (three eggs, one-eighth cup of milk, one-half cup diced ham, one-half cup diced onions, one-half cup diced green peppers, one-eighth cup diced cheddar cheese, a pinch of salt, and a dash of pepper), the tools needed (stove burner, large sauté pan, spatula, whisk, sharp knife, cutting board, plate), and the time needed (fifteen minutes preparation, five minutes cooking). You don't need to spend much time in your introduction covering these details, and you can skip over anything that's overly obvious or that might be better brought up later in the speech.

- *An effective demonstration speech includes, at its best, some element of audience participation:*

Just as audience members will perk up when a magician asks, "May I have a volunteer from the audience?" all audience members will be more focused if you invite their involvement. This can be done in three ways.

First, you might arrange with one or more audience member before the speech to act as an "assistant" by directly helping with the demonstration. (In this case, you have to guard against the potential drawback of the audience participation looking too "staged" or the assistant taking over. Be sure the assistant's role is clear to your helper before the speech beings.)

Second, you might ask for actual volunteers to take part in the process without any preparation. (The drawback with this method is that the volunteers might be slow or poorly skilled and slow down the demonstrations. Don't be shy about rushing them along if needed.)

Third, you might arrange for each member of the audience to have the supplies needed to do the process as the speaker demonstrates it. This can work especially well with a fairly simple speech that uses only a few inexpensive materials--making a paper airplane, for example. This strategy works best if you are willing to leave the front of the room and walk around through the audience—while still speaking—to oversee and help people as they do the process. (Of course, this can present many difficulties if the process is complicated or if supplies are limited. Also, some members of your audience may not be able to keep up with the steps, so you might have to move on and let them know that you can help them after the speech is over.)

Ultimately, though, any of these three methods can make the speech more entertaining for the audience by getting them involved in the process.

Most Common Problems with a Demonstration Speech

Rushing through demonstrations and not repeating steps for clarity: One of the easiest mistakes to make in a demonstration speech is to assume the audience understands the process the first time it is demonstrated. This is natural because the speaker is usually an expert at the process and understands each step very well. But you need to take on the viewpoint of the audience members who may not know anything about the process and may need each step to be demonstrated clearly and repeatedly for the process to be understood.

Not planning the demonstration to fit the time limits: Going significantly over or under the time limits for any speech is bad speechmaking, but that advice is especially important for a demonstration speech. Preparing and practicing ahead of time is essential for avoiding this problem. If you have five minutes to demonstrate a simple process, but you finish in two minutes, then you'll have a lot of time left to fill. In that case, it's best to slow the process down, repeat steps, or even repeat the whole process to make sure it is clear to the audience. Or if you get only halfway through a process and see the "one-minute-left" signal from your moderator, then that last minute will certainly be far too rushed. This problem can be solved by condensing some steps or by skipping them altogether by preparing several stages of the process ahead of time as is often done in cooking demonstration television shows. Also, keeping introductions and conclusions relatively brief keeps the focus on the steps in the process and helps you stay under the time limit.

Demonstration Speech Structure

In general, a demonstration speech should follow the basic structure shown below. (See the guidelines for organizing a speech in Section Three for basic information about how to structure a speech.)

- *Introduction:*
  Grabber
  Introduce the central theme of the speech
  Name and show the supplies needed
  Preview the main steps of the process

- *Body* (use this order for each main step in the process):

  Transition to the step
  Demonstrate the step
  Give important details about the step
  Repeat the demonstration and details if
      necessary

- *Conclusion:*
  Transition to the conclusion
  Re-emphasize the central theme of the speech
  Review the steps in the process
  Review the most important details about the
      process
  Closer

- *Introduction:*

  Grabber: Along with the traditional grabber methods detailed in Section Two, demonstration speeches often have physical objects that make natural grabbers. You will certainly get your audience interested in a speech about making brownies if you show them the finished product right at the end of the speech—particularly if that finished product is still warm and giving off a wonderful aroma and audience members are hungry! If the product of your demonstration doesn't smell as good as brownies do, you could also use a dramatic story about how you first became interested in the process as a grabber.

Introduce the central theme of the speech: On the surface, demonstration speeches would seem not to have a central theme beyond, "I'm going to show you how to do something." But the most effective demonstration speeches tell more than just "how to"; they make some kind of comment on the process being demonstrated. For example, the central theme of a speech demonstrating how to make a tie-dyed t-shirt in a microwave might be the "marriage of '60s pop culture and modern technology." Or a demonstration of how to make breakfast pizza might have a central theme that presents the topic as, "a great alternative to stale, leftover pizza from last night's party." A clear central theme can lift a demonstration to a higher level than one that just goes through the motions without a specific focus.

Name and show the supplies needed: Briefly let your audience know exactly what tools and supplies are needed, as well as how much time the process will take to complete. It's also a good idea to hold those tools and supplies up for the audience to see (if this is practical for your particular demonstration speech).

Preview the main steps of the process: Let your audience know the direction of the speech by letting them know the steps of the process at the end of your introduction. If there are only a few steps, list them: "Threading a needle involves preparing the thread, inserting the needle, and securing the thread to the needle." Or for a demonstration speech about making "breakfast pizza" (a speech with many steps), tell your audience that you will be taking them through the whole process, from preparing the ingredients, to baking, and finally to serving. (Note: previewing the main steps is different from listing the supplies needed—the steps are your main points, not the supplies.)

- *Body* (use this order for each main step in the process):

Transition to the step: Demonstration speeches most often have a very clear chronological order, so your transitions can usually be as simple as "first," "second," and "third." Make sure you stress these transitions so that your steps don't run the risk of blending together in your audience members' minds.

Demonstrate the step: For each step, you should tell and show exactly how the step is done. Make sure that your audience can see how you demonstrate the step and that you talk your way through the step and make lots of eye-contact as you demonstrate it. You can also slow down a step and show how to handle mistakes so that your audience is sure to follow the process.

Give important details about the step: Details about the steps should be integrated with your demonstrations. Some of these details might be essential information: "Unless you wait for the glue to dry before removing the clamps, the pieces will not bond together." Or the details could be fairly trivial tidbits that will both provide content and fill in the silence during demonstrations: "I generally use red or orange paint for the lettering to make the sign more visible, but other bold colors work well too."

Repeat the demonstration and details if necessary: Many demonstration speeches involve complicated topics, so it is often necessary to repeat demonstrations and details to assure that your audience has fully understood each step of the demonstration. There is nothing wrong with saying to your audience, "That was a fairly complex step, so let me show it to you again," or "Let me repeat this manufacturer's specification because it is essential that you use the right part in this step."

- *Conclusion*

Transition to the conclusion: Your audience will generally have a good idea that the demonstration speech is coming to a close because the process will be finished. But it is still a good idea to use a transition like "in conclusion" as a further signal that the speech is about to end.

Re-emphasize the central theme of the speech: At the end of the demonstration speech, the audience will have the full extent of the process as context, so the central theme will be even clearer to them when you re-emphasize it as part of your conclusion. For example, "Remember that you don't need any special training beyond what I've just showed you to start playing the kazoo."

Review the steps in the process: If the process is simple and brief with only a few steps, then run through those steps again quickly to give your audience one last refresher. If the process is long and complicated, summarize the steps to tie the process together clearly.

Review the most important details about the process:
Some details about the process are so important that they bear repeating at the end of the speech to make sure that the audience has no chance to forget them. This is particularly true of details about safety: "Please, whatever you do, for everyone's safety, make sure that the unit is unplugged before you begin working on the wiring."

Closer: A call to action is often the most natural and effective closer for a demonstration speech because you can send the audience off to try the process for themselves. Dramatic statements also work well: "With the knowledge that you now have about CPR, you will never be faced with the prospect of standing around while a loved one is at the brink of death from heart failure."

Demonstration Speech Practice Assignment

Demonstrate how to do a specific process. Your two primary goals will be to show your audience how the process works and teach them enough to try the process themselves. You should have some expertise at doing this process so that you can focus on presenting the speech rather than learning the process for yourself. Be sure to select a topic that you can demonstrate effectively without going over or under the time limits.

Persuasion Speech

What is a Persuasion Speech?

A persuasion speech explains an issue and attempts to get an audience to agree with the speaker's position on that issue—or, if agreement is unlikely, at least to respect the speaker's opinion on the issue.

Key Public Speaking Skills Needed for a Persuasion Speech

Explaining an issue and influencing the attitudes, values, beliefs, and actions of audience members who may or may not agree with the speaker's position on that issue.

Examples of Persuasion Speeches

- a teenager tries to persuade her parents that she should have a car
- a political candidate tries to persuade voters that they should vote for her
- a student attempts to convince a teacher that a poem holds a certain meaning
- an employee gives a presentation about changing an outdated sales approach
- a trainer tells a coach why her team should do more weight lifting

The Qualities of an Effective Persuasion Speech

- *An effective persuasion speech clearly explains the issue being considered:*

People use the term "issue" often, but its meaning isn't always clear. An *issue* is an idea or notion about which reasonable people disagree. Our world is full of issues, from politics and religion all the way down to personal choices. Taxes and life after death are issues, but so are things like exercise and clothing. Whenever reasonable people disagree, an issue exists.

Persuasion speeches are centered on issues. But before you can *influence* the audience members' positions on an issue, you must first make sure that the audience *understands* the issue. Without audience understanding, reaching agreement on or earning respect about an issue is unlikely. And while it may seem that "winning" is the ultimate goal of persuasion, simply winning the debate without increasing your audience's understanding of the issue is a very hollow victory. (One reason many people dislike politicians, for example, is that they too often fail to explain issues or even purposely confuse issues. When a politician talks about cutting taxes but doesn't explain what service would be cut as well, that makes for very hollow persuasion. This inattention to issue explanation partly explains low voter turnout in many American elections.)

Explaining the issue can often take place in the introduction of the speech, especially if the issue isn't very complex. Or explanatory details can be parceled out in the body of the speech and interwoven with the main points. Outside the world of politics, if you are trying to persuade your audience that weightlifting is a better form of exercise than jogging, for example, then you need to define exactly what sort of weightlifting program or jogging routine you have in mind. Or if the issue under consideration is what destinations make for he best vacations, then you have to explain all relevant information, from hidden costs to potential unexpected travel problems.

- *An effective persuasion speech has a definite position on a specific issue:*

In life, the best position on an issue sometimes seems to be a combination of positions. Life can often measured in shades of gray rather than in stark contrasts. But in terms of persuasive speaking, this does not mean that you shouldn't have a definite position. A persuasive speech about a healthy diet, for example, could take a vegan position, or that a high-protein diet composed primarily of red meat will prevent muscle atrophy in middle and old age, or that a balance of fruits, vegetables, and meat is best—just so the position is clear and specific.

Whatever the specific position, you must be definitely and clearly *in favor* of that position or *against* certain opposing positions. Persuasive speeches should explain an issue so that the audience understands that issue, but they should not simply present facts about an issue and hope the audience will come to a correct position. We might be tempted to assume that our audience will come to the best position if we only present facts in a neutral way, but that usually isn't the case. Persuasion speeches should present facts and show the audience how these facts lead to lead to the best position.

The issue should also be as specific as possible. Instead of a speech that attempts to persuade an audience that a presidential candidate is a good person (a person's "goodness" being a very vague issue), a speech addressing a more specific issue—such as why a candidate's specific policy platform is good for the country—would be better because policy platform is a more specific issue than a measure of "goodness."

- *An effective persuasion speech presents clear, appropriate reasons for the position and convincing, well-developed, specific evidence for each reason:*

The building blocks of a sound persuasion speech are reasons why the audience should hold a certain position on an issue. *Reasons* are the answers to the question "why?" when you state your position on an issue. While reasons are the overarching main points of a persuasion speech, *evidence* constitutes the particular details that develop, illustrate, and support those reasons. Reasons give an argument depth; evidence gives an argument weight.

For example, a speech persuading an audience to eat at one restaurant rather than another might present these reasons in favor of the preferred restaurant to answer the question "Why is this restaurant better than the other ones?": better food, more variety of food choices, better service, better prices, better atmosphere, and more convenient location. These reasons would comprise the main points of the speech, be presented one at a time with the most important first, be emphasized very clearly during the speech, and be listed on a handout for the audience.

If one reason in a speech persuading an audience to choose one restaurant over another is that the first restaurant has better service, then the speaker must present evidence of that better service—descriptions of the behavior and attitudes of servers, the time it takes to get waited on and for food to arrive, reviews and ratings of the service from various online sites, etc. For a reason stating that the preferred restaurant has more variety of food choices, the evidence might consist of a close comparison of the two restaurants' menus, showing the greater selection available at the better restaurant.

(Note: *Research* on your topic—from traditional library/internet research to your own field research—is a key activity for developing an understanding of an issue and for discovering reasons and evidence to support your position in a persuasive speech.)

- *An effective persuasion speech includes an acknowledgement or counterargument of other sides of the issue:*

If a you ignore the other sides of an issue, the audience might believe you're concealing important points and lose faith in your objectivity and credibility. But if a you present too much of the other sides of an issue, the audience might be confused about what your position actually is. So the goal is something in between—either an acknowledgement or counterargument of the opposition's important points.

For example, if you are trying to persuade an audience that one football team is likely to beat its opponent in an upcoming game, but the opposing team clearly has a better quarterback, you could *acknowledge* that point by noting it in the speech—but then showing that the quarterback's particular skills won't be the most important factor in an upcoming game. Even though the opposing quarterback may be better, his team might not have the receivers to take full advantage of his skills. Your favored team may not have as strong a quarterback, but your team might have a better running game and the short-pass receivers to make the overall offense more successful.

Or the speaker may *counterargue* the point that the opposing team has a better quarterback by claiming that, despite the common wisdom, your quarterback is actually better, then citing key statistics or plays that serve as evidence to prove your quarterback's superiority.

Counterarguments can be woven into your reasons and evidence as they naturally come up, or they can be dealt with in separate body sections. A useful guideline to follow is that if you believe your audience generally agrees with your position or is mostly neutral, then summarize your counterarguments near the end of the speech, sort of as a final main point. If your audience tends to disagree with your position, then you might try organizing the whole speech around counterarguments, using an outline of all the objects the audience members have to your position as the framework for the body of the speech.

When looking at the other sides of an issue, you must examine perspectives different from your own. This can be very difficult, especially when you believe very strongly that your side of the issue is right. But instead of simply dismissing other views, you have to honestly, objectively, and respectfully show why other people might disagree with you about the issue. And you need to take on the opposition's *best* reasons, not a "straw-man" argument against the easiest ones or ones that misrepresent opposing views. When you fully understand views other than your own, you can then effectively take these views into account in your persuasive speech. (Or you might even change your position based on learning more, and then change your entire speech. Even in today's hard-line world, change is possible.)

- *An effective persuasion speech displays a respectful tone and emotional appeal:*

Although you may disagree with people holding opposing viewpoints on an issue, you shouldn't let your tone show anything but respect for the opposition. A respectful tone is the equivalent of keeping one's voice under control in a heated discussion. Shouting or screaming at another person in a discussion is disrespectful, just as belittling the opposing side in a persuasion speech shows disrespect. In short, don't use the comment boards on political websites as your model for persuasive speaking. These anonymous outlets are full of people working out their own psychological issues by being purposefully disrespectful to anyone they disagree with—but they seldom lead to any understanding or persuasion about the issues they address.

You may sometimes have no chance of getting an audience to agree with your position (for example, a movie distributor trying to get the programming committee of a religious television station to show the movie *Dogma*), but that speaker should never be disrespectful of the audience. When you realize that agreement is unlikely, then your goal for the speech should become simply getting the audience to respect your position. In other words, the goal becomes getting the audience to believe that you are honestly an intelligent person with good intentions and not an evil person with a destructive agenda. Many politicians turn off voters because they can't keep a respectful tone when speaking about their opponents.

Making emotional appeals connects with establishing a respectful tone by helping the audience want to accept the speaker's position. While the respectful tone helps the audience believe in your good qualities as a person, emotional appeals help the audience believe in the good qualities of your position. Emotional appeals help the audience see that they will *feel* good or moral or right about agreeing with the speaker's position.

For example, if your want to persuade audience members to be involved with the local activities of Habitat for Humanity (a group that builds housing for the poor), your could show examples of specific families who were helped by the organization, possibly even showing photos of these families in the homes that Habitat for Humanity helped them build. Along with understanding the logical reasons and evidence that Habitat for Humanity helps people, the audience members will also *feel* how good providing that help is because it helps actual human beings, further persuading them to adopt your position.

Most Common Problems with a Persuasion Speech

Not having a sound argument for your position: Some attempts to be persuasive depend too much on emotional appeal and not enough on the reasons and evidence that create a sound argument. For example, a politician trying to win audience members' votes by promising tax cuts might settle for just the emotional appeal of voters paying less hard-earned income in taxes. But that candidate will not be as persuasive as one who advocates the same tax cuts, but goes beyond just the emotional appeal and presents reasons and evidence to show that the tax cut will not deplete essential government services that taxpayers rely on.

Offending your audience or making them feel stupid or bad: If a speaker talks down to an audience in any way, that speaker undermines the message that he or she is trying to convey, especially in terms of persuasive speaking. For example, if you want to persuade smokers to quit smoking, you should not present medical evidence of the harm of smoking as if the audience has never heard of it. Of course they've heard it before. The audience members will think that you consider them ignorant of this basic information.

Or if you "lectures" the audience on how "everyone knows" that smoking is bad for their general health, or that only a "self-destructive idiot" would smoke, then the audience members will feel they are being unfairly punished and will naturally rebel against your position—whether or not they are smokers or non-smokers. You would have much better luck with a speech that gave the audience new information about smoking as part of the speech's reasons and evidence or that had the emotional appeal of empathy and understanding the difficulties involved in quitting smoking.

Persuasion Speech Structure

In general, a persuasion speech should follow the basic structure shown below. (See the guidelines for organizing a speech in Section Three for basic information about how to structure a speech.)

- *Introduction:*
  - Grabber
  - Define the issue
  - State your position on the issue
  - Preview the reasons for your position

- *Body* (use this order for each reason for your position):
  - Transition to the reason for your position
  - State (and emphasize) the reason for your position
  - Provide evidence (specific details) to support the reason for your position

- *Conclusion:*
  - Transition to the conclusion
  - Re-emphasize your position of the issue
  - Review the reasons for your position
  - Closer

- *Introduction:*

   Grabber: The grabber for a persuasion speech is especially important because persuasion is a form of communication that can sometimes lead to audience alienation. An audience that might disagree with you could be antagonistic, while an audience that agrees with you might be a bit apathetic. So the grabber must energize the audience by making the issue as concrete and real as possible (without simply lapsing into sensationalism). Dramatic statements of fact or anecdotes can work particularly well. For example, a speech that focuses on persuading an audience to support gun safety training programs might present the annual number of accidental gun deaths or tell the story of a specific accidental gun death to capture the audience's interest.

   Define the issue: If your audience doesn't know much about the issue, you will have to give them any needed background information. This could be done objectively (without stacking the deck in favor of your position), clearly, and concisely early in the speech to be certain that your audience understands exactly what the issue is and what its implications are. Being concise is especially important when defining the issue early in the speech because you will want to move on to the important reasons and evidence in the body of the speech (where you may also include some explanation of the issue as well).

   State your position on the issue: The central theme of a persuasion speech is a combination of the issue and your position. Everything in the speech will in some way support your position on the issue, which should be clearly stated in the introduction so that the audience knows that position early in the speech. Speakers are sometimes tempted to hold off revealing their position until late in the speech, hoping to build their position as an inevitable conclusion based on the facts presented. Only very skilled and experienced public speakers are able to be persuasive while using such as structure. Persuasive speaking is almost always clearer and more convincing when the position is revealed in the introduction rather than held for the conclusion.

Preview the reasons for your position: If you have only a few reasons, list them at the end of the introduction: for example, "There are four main reasons why Daryl Barone would make a strong student body president: his experience in student government, his internship in the state senate, his commitment to students having access to the college governance structures, and his connections with the college's board of trustees." On the other hand, longer, more complicated speeches may have a large number of reasons for a position. In that case, simply summarize those reasons as you conclude your introduction: "The new tax law is bad for our citizens because of reasons ranging from the law's many loopholes to the difficult new tax forms associated with the law."

- *Body* (use this order for each reason for your position):

Transition to the reason for your position: Transitions in a persuasion speech often focus on the importance of each particular reason. Usually, the best way to order main points is from most to least important, so your transitions should reflect that order. You might move from the introduction to your first main point with a transition such as, "First, let's consider the most important reason to buy a home gym." The transition to the second main point might be something like this: "The second reason to purchase a home gym may not be as obvious as the first reason, but it is still a very significant point."

State and emphasize the reason for your position: When you give a reason for your position as a main point in your speech, be sure to present that reason clearly and simply and to emphasize the point strongly. You shouldn't brush over your reasons and assume your audience will "get" them. And you shouldn't just say something vague like, "Another thing is ..." These reasons may be clear to you because you believe in them strongly and you have been rehearsing them as part of your speech preparation for weeks. But your audience needs clear statements and strong emphasis to digest the reasons and to gain a sense of the authority you bring to your position.

Provide evidence (specific details) to support the reason for your position: A list of reasons, no matter how clear and strong they may be, probably will not convince your audience that your position is the way to go. Just as a lawyer must present a substantial amount of evidence to convince a jury of a client's innocence, a persuasive speaker must develop reasons with specific details that support those reasons. If you have lots of time for a speech, provide lots of detail in clear, reasonable, interesting ways. If your speech is brief, make sure that the limited amount of evidence that you present within the time frame is the most important, most convincing evidence that you have available. And definitely do not be afraid to include research information as part of your evidence.

- *Conclusion:*

Transition to the conclusion: The old favorite, "in conclusion," is fine, but a persuasive speech might also follow that up with something like, "I hope the reasons and evidence that I've presented will lead you to the conclusion that ... (insert your position on the issue here)."

Re-emphasize your position of the issue: Come back to the central theme of the speech (your position on the issue) to re-focus your audience's attention back to what is most important—exactly what you are trying to persuade them to think or feel or believe or do.

Review the reasons for your position: List or summarize your reasons one final time to guarantee as much clarity as you can for your speech.

Closer: Because persuasion speeches are sometimes rousing for the audience, a call to action can work well for a closer. A candidate for public office might call out, "So I need your vote in November to make these changes possible!" But any form of closer can also be effective, as long as it is delivered strongly and reaffirms your position on the issue in a dramatic way that gives the speech a powerful finish.

Persuasion Speech
Practice Assignment

Find an issue that is important to you and that reasonable people disagree about, briefly explain that issue, take a definite position on that issue, and try to persuade your audience to agree with your position primarily through reasons and evidence. (If you believe that agreement from your audience is impossible, then try to get them to respect your position, even if they disagree.) Your issue may be as big as national politics or religion, or as small as personal preference. (These topics should be avoided because they are usually too complex or emotional for a practice class assignment: war, abortion, welfare, smoking, gun control, and capital punishment. Outside of class, when you have less-restrictive time limits and more experience with public speaking, these are powerful, meaningful topics worth exploring.)

Impromptu Speech

What is an Impromptu Speech?

An impromptu speech responds in a coherent, organized, well-presented way (usually briefly) to a question or topic where the speaker has little or no preparation time.

Key Public Speaking Skills Needed for an Impromptu Speech

Quickly organizing and delivering material in an efficient, goal-oriented way.

Examples of Impromptu Speeches

- a speaker responds to audience questions after a prepared speech
- a student answers a teacher's question in class
- a prospective employee responds to questions during a job interview
- an organization member gives a brief report on an activity at a group meeting
- an elected official responds to reporters' questions while on vacation

The Qualities of an Effective Impromptu Speech

- *An effective impromptu speech involves calm, unruffled, public speaking performance:*

While you can't generate much of the content of an impromptu speech before the speech itself, and you'll have to prepare that content very quickly with little or no time, you still know long before speaking that *performance* will be a very important element of the speech. So constant practice and awareness of effective public speaking performance skills (voice, eye-contact, body language, and "personality" put into the speech) can lead to stronger impromptu speeches.

For example, if you are asked to give a report at an organizational meeting, you may have to come up with main points and details on the spot, but your mind should automatically be focused on projecting your voice to be heard easily by people at the meeting, making eye-contact to connect with those present at the meeting, using gestures to emphasize important points of the content, and investing your report with authority, professionalism, and enthusiasm.

- *An effective impromptu speech utilizes extremely quick preparation:*

If you finds out that you have 15 minutes to prepare an impromptu speech, then your mind should be strongly focused on the speech preparation during those 15 minutes, perhaps jotting down notes and mentally rehearsing as much as possible. Or if you are asked to speak right away, then you should take whatever seconds are available to prepare. The key aspect of preparing an impromptu speech quickly is focusing your concentration on generating the content, rather than on worrying about matters that are out of your control—such as how little preparation time you have.

For example, if a student is called on randomly to answer a question in class, only the most mean-spirited instructor would not allow that student a few seconds of relative silence to prepare a thoughtful response.

- *An effective impromptu speech uses a pre-set organizational structure:*

Impromptu speeches can be prepared most efficiently if they are structured exactly like a regular speech (introduction, body, conclusion—see the impromptu speech structure below). If you internalize this structure and use it every time you make an impromptu speech, then the structure will be taken care of in advance, and you can focus on quickly developing content to fill out that structure—rather than rambling because of the pressure of an impromptu situation.

For example, if a candidate for a job is asked why he or she is interested in a job, the candidate knows that the response should start with an introduction ("I've wanted to work as an outdoor guide since I first went to camp as a child"), move on to a few main points in the body ("Being an outdoor guide keeps me involved in the three things I've always enjoyed: nature, travel, and outdoor sports"), and then provide a basic conclusion ("So those three reasons make being an outdoor guide an ideal career for me.")

Being organized in the high-pressure situation of an impromptu speech can be especially impressive to your audience because we are all used to seeing people respond poorly in these situations and give rambling or rushed speeches.

- *An effective impromptu speech is organized around a few clear, well-emphasized main points with appropriate details:*

Just as main points create the structure of any speech, an impromptu speech also relies on main points. These main points form the body of the speech and are compromised of the big ideas that you want the audience to remember when the speech is finished. And you must emphasize these points to give the speech a rhythm and flow, as well as to aid the audience in remembering each point. The fact that a speech is impromptu is no reason that it should ramble.

In the example from the job interview described above, the body of the impromptu speech contains three main points: "Being an outdoor guide keeps me involved in three things I've always enjoyed: nature, travel, and outdoor sports." These three main points would be previewed near the beginning of the speech, emphasized clearly at one time in the body of the speech, and developed with appropriate details (depending on the time available for the speech).

- *An effective impromptu speech has strong openings and closings:*

Although an impromptu speech allows little time for preparation, you should always know that an impromptu speech must have a grabber to get the audience's attention and a closer to tie the speech together. And because an audience sometimes expects an impromptu speaker to not be prepared, having a good grabber and closer can be especially impressive. Impromptu speakers might rely on a quick wit for instant impromptu grabbers and closers, but not everyone can be that creative. So speakers often have a pre-set selection of grabbers and closers at their disposal to adapt to a specific impromptu speaking situation.

For example, when taking impromptu questions after a prepared speech relating to movies, a speaker can anticipate what some of the questions might be like and have a grabber about how high the price of admission has become at movie theaters. The speaker can then adapt that pre-selected grabber to any question, such as, "What is the best movie you've seen this year?" (Grabber: "Well, with the price of admission being so high, I've only been able to see one movie this year, so I guess it was the best!") Or the question might be, "Why does it cost so much to make movies these days?" (Grabber: "Because Hollywood production companies have to do something to justify the high admission prices at the theaters.") A pre-selected closer can work the same way—in this example, perhaps by framing the impromptu response by connecting the beginning and ending with a comment about the high price of popcorn and snacks at the theater.

Most Common Problems
with an Impromptu Speech

Panicking, freezing, or rushing because of a momentary mental block: The pressure of public speaking in general is compounded by the need to think fast when doing an impromptu speech specifically. So the dreaded "mental block" (sometimes colorfully called a "brain fart") can be even more common during an impromptu speech than any other kind of speaking task. But panicking or freezing in this situation will bring disappointment from your audience at worst and pity at best—neither of which is a desired audience response to effective public speaking. The best way to avoid mental blocks is by doing as much limited preparation as is possible in the limited time you have: using the pre-set structure, having grabbers and closers, emphasizing performance skills, etc.

If a mental block does occur during your impromptu speech, you should try to remember where you were in the speech structure: Still in your introduction? On a main point or detail? In the conclusion? If you can't remember for sure, take your best guess and pick up from that point. You may notice that the speech went off course, but chances are good that your audience won't know the difference.

Impromptu speeches should also not automatically be assumed to be short speeches. While a short response in an impromptu speaking situation often gets to the point well enough, audiences usually require at least some elaboration to fully understand the point. In addition, too many brief responses to impromptu questions (such as during a job interview) might lead to 15 minutes of speaking when a full hour has been allotted, perhaps giving the impression that the speaker is either unprepared, under-knowledgeable, or simply not an effective communicator. (Of course, long-windedness should be avoided as well.)

Fabricating a less-than-knowledgeable response to a question: One of the biggest public speaking fears is that someone will ask us a question that leaves us completely stumped. Unfortunately, that situation happens to almost every public speaker now and then. The temptation when this happens is to make something up to avoid sounding ignorant to your audience. But this strategy can lead to all sorts of trouble, especially if your fabrication is discovered by the audience.

The best strategy to adopt when you don't know the answer to a question is to say, "That's a great question. I haven't considered that perspective. I don't know the answer." Then offer to research the information and get back to the questioner. In a job interview, for example, make a note of the question, and then include the answer in your follow-up letter or e-mail to the potential employers after the interview.

Impromptu Speech Structure

In general, an impromptu speech should follow the basic structure shown below. Even when you have very limited preparation time, following a structure like this will guard against the "babbling" or "rambling" that impromptu speeches are sometimes prone to. (See the guidelines for organizing a speech in Section Three for basic information about how to structure a speech.)

- *Introduction:*
    - Grabber
    - Introduce the central theme of the speech
    - Preview the main points

- *Body* (use this order for each main point):
    - Transition to the main point
    - State and emphasize the main point
    - Provide necessary details about the main point

- *Conclusion:*
    - Transition to the conclusion
    - Re-emphasize the central theme of the speech
    - Review the main points
    - Closer

- *Introduction:*

Grabber: A snappy beginning can get an impromptu speech off to an unexpectedly strong start. The pre-formulated grabber can be effective because you don't have to rely on your wits quite as much.

Introduce the central theme of the speech: No matter how brief or last-second an impromptu speech might be, it should still have a central theme. That theme will usually grow out of the larger context of the impromptu situation—for example, an impromptu response to every question at a job interview has the central theme that you are a good choice for the job. Working such a theme in to the impromptu speech in a subtle way can focus your audience. A job interview question that asks about your work background can elicit an impromptu response with this central theme, made clear by the larger situation of the job interview: "My previous experience in sales has been a solid preparation for work in your marketing department."

Preview the main points: Because impromptu speeches are usually brief, you will probably have only a few main points. But it is still important to preview those main points. For example, "The two easiest ways to mess up when using this machine are miscalculations of time and size matching." This preview prepares the audience for the body of the response, and it helps you stay on track rather than ramble though the impromptu speech.

• *Body:*

Transition to the main point: Transitions between main points guard against a disjointed speech body, something that can easily happen under the natural pressures of giving an impromptu speech. Simple transitions ("first," "second," "third"; "most important," "less important," etc.) often are best to shape the body of an impromptu speech given with very limited preparation and under lots of pressure.

State and emphasize the main point: Clearly stated, strongly emphasized main points will invest the body of an impromptu speech with organization and authority greater than a speech that merely glosses over its main points.

Provide necessary details about the main point: Some impromptu speeches may be very brief (20-30 seconds, for instance, when responding to one of many questions after a prepared speech) that there is no time for any real detail. But whatever detail you can inject to illustrate your main points will make the impromptu speech more fully developed and clearer than a simple list of main points.

- *Conclusion*

Transition to the conclusion: This is one type of speech where the traditional "in conclusion" may not work well because you may be responding to several impromptu questions in a row (at a job interview, for example), and you don't want to repeat "in conclusion" many times in a row at the end of a series of brief responses. Instead, alternating among a variety of transitions such as, "summing up," "pulling these points together," or "the bottom line is…" will work better.

Re-emphasize the central theme of the speech: Touching on the central theme again will keep it in focus—as long as you are not too repetitive in a very brief impromptu response.

Review the main points: Referring to the main points again can give them the emphasis and clarity needed to make them memorable for your audience—again, as long as you are careful to avoid being overly repetitive in a short impromptu speech.

Closer: Just as having a good grabber is unexpected but welcome in an impromptu speech, so is having a strong closer to end the speech. Pre-selected closers can work well, or you might like to let your closer develop from the direction that the impromptu response takes as you deliver it.

Impromptu Speech
Practice Assignment

Respond to a topic using very little preparation time. You will be given a few minutes to prepare responses to several potential topics, and then one topic will be selected at random for your impromptu speech. All of the potential topics will be unknown to you in advance, but they will be familiar enough to prepare a response from your own knowledge and experience without doing any outside research. You will be given a preset organizational pattern to assist you in your preparation.

Manuscript Speech

What is a Manuscript Speech?

A manuscript speech involves presenting a previously written text to an audience in such a way that the presentation mirrors and amplifies the meaning of the text.

Key Public Speaking Skills Needed for a Manuscript Speech

Investing appropriate personality into scripted text, especially text written by someone other than the speaker.

Examples of Manuscript Speeches

- a supervisor reads a memo from the company president to a group of employees
- a family member reads a letter from a distant relative at a family reunion
- a politician reads a speech written by a speech writer
- a grade school teacher reads to children from a book of fables
- an author reads from her latest work to a group of her fans

The Qualities of an Effective Manuscript Speech

- *An effective manuscript speech is invested with appropriate emotion and emphasis:*

We have all sat through dull manuscript speeches. Because of its reliance on the actual printed word, no other speech type is as prone to becoming boring as manuscript reading. The key to making a manuscript reading interesting for your audience is bringing some personality to it. The technical term for this is *interpretation.* You need to discern the tone of the manuscript (happy, sad, serious, comic, etc.) and bring an emotional interpretation to the reading that matches that tone. You also need to discover the main points of the manuscript (which are not always made clear by the author) and stress those main points by speaking them with more force and bringing appropriate body language and gestures to those points.

For example, a speaker at the dedication of a new building who has been asked to read a proclamation letter from the state governor must adopt the emotional tone of the manuscript (celebratory and formal) and emphasize the important points of the manuscript (how much the community has supported the project and how much the project will mean to the community).

- *An effective manuscript speech maintains a well-presented overall public speaking performance:*

Manuscript readings seem on the surface like they would be easy to present, but they are actually the hardest speeches to present (especially for inexperienced speakers). Demonstrating the basic qualities of good public speaking performance is very difficult when reading from a manuscript. Especially difficult are maintaining eye-contact with the audience and projecting your voice out to the audience while reading. These two aspects of public speaking performance need to be stressed as much as possible.

For example, a scientist at a professional conference reading a report on the results of her experiment needs to lift her head from the report to look at the audience as much as possible and send her voice out to that audience rather than down into the report itself where her voice would be muffled. The key for that scientist is to know her report "backward and forward." She needs to practice reading it many times, be sure of how to pronounce the technical terms, and be clear about the overall direction of the report. She will then know the report so well that she will only need to glance down at it a few times during her reading while keeping her eyes and voice focused on connecting with her audience.

- *An effective manuscript speech involves reading the text smoothly and carefully:*

When you read a manuscript, you should not have to stumble over words or try to decipher meanings as you read to your audience. You should understand the manuscript clearly long before you have to present it. The best way to achieve a smooth reading is through repeated practice.

For example, if you are a manager who has to read a memo from the company president to employees in your division, you must find a private place (your office, your car, an empty restroom, etc.) to re-read that memo many times. The re-reading should be both silent—to assure your familiarity with the memo's content—and, especially, aloud—to assure your comfort with the wording and points of emphasis.

- *An effective manuscript speech clearly introduces the material being read:*

No matter how self-explanatory a manuscript might be, you will probably need to introduce it briefly to your audience before actually reading it. Just as with any other speech, a grabber that gets your audience's attention is a good way to begin. Other key elements to the introduction of a manuscript reading are naming and describing the manuscript and its author.

For example, a teacher reading a children's book called *Alexander and the Terrible, Horrible, No Good, Very Bad Day* by Judith Viorst might describe some things that typically happen to children on a "bad" day (siblings getting them in trouble, toy breaking, parent forgetting an important soccer game, etc.). This grabber would get the children interested in the general topic of the manuscript. The teacher could then show them the book, tell the children the title and author, and then explain that he or she is reading it to show the children that all kids have bad days now and then. Such an introduction would help the children enjoy the reading more than if the teacher had just started reading from the book without a preamble.

- *An effective manuscript speech concludes with an indication of how the audience should use the information presented:*

Just as the manuscript reading will be clearer when the material is introduced before it is read, the reading should also conclude with information on what the material means to the particular audience.

For example, a fast food chain manager reading a memo from the "central office" about a new sales procedure would conclude with a review of the procedure and a discussion of how it could be implemented at this particular restaurant. The manager could then give the workers a call to action as a closer to the speech.

Most Common Problems with a Manuscript Speech

Not investing the reading with the appropriate personality: When you read a manuscript without emotion or emphasis, not only is it boring to the audience, but the material loses a great deal of the meaning that can be conveyed through an effective speaker's emotion and emphasis. Lost meaning can lead to misunderstandings, missed connections, and many general communication problems that could be avoided by bringing your personality to the reading.

Not maintaining eye-contact with the audience or not projecting your voice to the audience: As two of the essential components of public speaking performance, eye-contact and projection of voice can make or break any speech—especially one that involves reading from a manuscript. Looking down at the manuscript throughout the reading sends the audience three messages: that you don't care about them, that you don't know the material, and that you are something of a bumbler overall. And sending your voice down into the manuscript instead of out to the audience not only muffles your voice to the point where your audience might not hear you, but also sends many of the same negative messages as not making eye-contact with your audience.

Manuscript Speech Structure

In general, a manuscript speech should follow the basic structure shown below. (See the guidelines for organizing a speech in Section Three for basic information about how to structure a speech.)

- *Introduction:*
  - Grabber
  - Identify the material and the author
  - Explain why you are reading the manuscript
  - Preview the content

- *Body:*
  - Transition to reading the manuscript
  - Read the manuscript
  - Repeat any essential passages (if necessary)
  - Explain the manuscript (if necessary)

- *Conclusion:*
  - Transition to the conclusion
  - Review the content

- Re-emphasize the importance and meaning of the manuscript
- Closer

• *Introduction:*

Grabber: Having a grabber may seem strange for a manuscript speech because the primary focus of the speech will be reading from a manuscript. But getting your audience's attention with a strong grabber is actually more important for a manuscript speech than any other type of speech. Audience members will have a natural tendency to assume they will be bored when they know someone is about to read to them because the usual reading can be pretty dull. But a strong grabber, closely related to the manuscript content, will let your audience know that this manuscript reading will be something different—something that holds their attention.

Identify the material and author: The extent of the identifying information depends on the situation. If you are reading a memo from the boss, and the boss is familiar to everyone in the audience, then you don't need to say much about the material or author. But if you are reading a passage from a novel to a class that may not be familiar with the author or her novel, you would want to give some background on the author and the novel itself.

Explain why you are reading the manuscript: Most manuscript speeches have a clear purpose. That purpose might be to give people essential information to help them do their jobs, to give news from a far-off relative or friend, or simply to entertain them with a good story. Letting your audience know the specific purpose helps them know how to process the information in the manuscript.

Preview the content: Because you will have read the manuscript closely before reading it to your audience, you will know the central theme and main points of that manuscript. Previewing that content might include giving a summary of the manuscript, a list of its main points, or directions about what aspects of the manuscript the audience should pay the most attention to during the reading. The key element of the preview is giving the audience the context needed to understand the manuscript as clearly as possible.

- *Body:*

Transition to reading the manuscript: You want to make sure that your audience knows exactly where your introduction ends and your reading of the actual manuscript begins. This will be revealed mostly through your public speaking performance: you will change from speaking extemporaneously to reading. But a clear transition—such as, "I'll begin reading at this point," or simply saying "quote" as you begin quoting, along with a strong pause before you actually begin reading—will further guide your listeners.

Read the manuscript: Read your manuscript clearly, and remember to invest your reading with strong performance skills: voice, eye-contact, body language, and personality.

Repeat any essential passages (if necessary): Your audience will appreciate hearing the truly essential portions of the manuscript again, so you should go back and re-read what is most important. Preface your re-

reading with a transition such as, "Let me go back and read this important part again to make sure that it's clear."

Explain the manuscript (if necessary): Some parts of the manuscript may need amplification and explanation. You should try to anticipate the questions your audience will have about any unclear portions of the manuscript and then try to answer those questions even before the audience asks them. It's usually okay to interrupt your actual manuscript reading here and there for such explanations.

- *Conclusion:*

Transition to the conclusion: The standard transition, "in conclusion," is acceptable here, or any signal to your audience that the speech is nearing its finish. Your audience will probably be able to see when you move from reading to speaking extemporaneously, so the transition here is usually pretty apparent.

Review the content: Review the content to be sure that it is as clear as possible for the audience by summarizing or listing the main points of the manuscript.

Re-emphasize the importance and meaning of the manuscript: Once more, restate the essence of the manuscript, exactly why it was important enough to be read aloud and what its implications are beyond the present moment.

Closer: A call to action often works well at the end of the manuscript speech, especially when the manuscript itself is some sort of call to action, such as a memo form a manager about a new productivity goal. Any sort of closer, however, is better than simply saying something like, "Okay, that's it."

Manuscript Speech
Practice Assignment

Select a text to read aloud. The text could be
anything—from a poem, song lyrics, scene from a play,
part of a novel or short story, to a memo, scientific
textbook, newspaper article, or the text of someone
else's speech. (For this assignment, it is better not to
select something that you wrote yourself so that you
can practice interpreting an unfamiliar manuscript.)
Introduce the material to the audience, read it
effectively, showing appropriate emotion and
enthusiasm and strong public speaking performance
skills, and conclude it.

About the Author

John Sheirer is an award-winning author and teacher who has given thousands of speeches in his career. He has been teaching public speaking for many years at Asnuntuck Community College in Enfield, Connecticut. He still gets a little nervous before each speech.